I0796719

101 REASONS WHY I LOVE THE NBA

First published in the UK by Sona Books, an imprint of Danann Media Publishing Limited

CAT NO. SON0614

Cover and book design: Darren Grice & Kevin Gardner

Editor: Martin Corteel

Proof reader: Cameron Thurlow

Printed in EU

ISBN: 978-1-915343-78-9

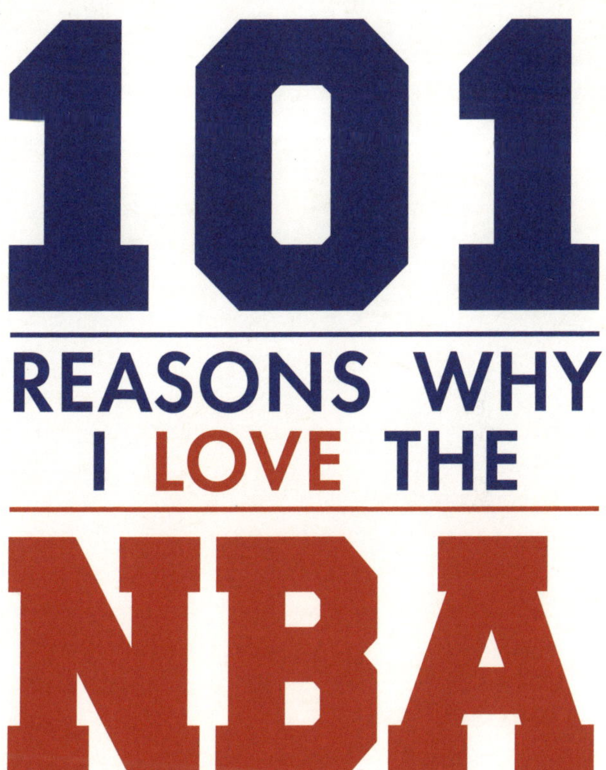

101 REASONS WHY I LOVE THE NBA

SCOTT REEVES

INTRODUCTION

The NBA has a claim to be America's biggest export. Around 800 million people follow the premier pro basketball league in some form, making it the fourth most popular sporting competition in the world, behind only football, tennis and the Olympics. It's a truly global league, with high numbers of fans in Brazil, China, Spain, Australia and South Africa.

It's not hard to see what attracts so many fans. There's wall-to-wall action, with 48 minutes of live play on the clock. Compare that to 17 minutes of play in a three-hour baseball game, or just 11 minutes of action in the NFL. Basketball players are phenomenal athletes, and every man on the roster needs to contribute in every aspect of the game. There are no specialised pitchers or designated hitters in basketball, and no separate offensive and defensive units. Whether they're a guard, forward or centre, every basketball player needs to be comfortable shooting, blocking, rebounding and assisting.

For more than 75 years, the NBA has thrilled its fans. It's been the stage upon which some of the most recognisable sport stars in history have performed: we're looking at you, **Michael Jordan** and LeBron James. It's seen some amazing games, from Malice in the Palace to

Wilt Chamberlain's unbeatable 100-pointer. The NBA is also America's most diverse pro sports league and leads the way in uniting a country that's fragmented on so many other levels.

Join us as we discover the 101 reasons why the NBA isn't just one of the most popular sports leagues in the world, but is a cultural phenomenon.

KOCH
WIZARDS
If he MISSES
ETIHAD
Verizon Center

78
1943 1982 1984
1985 2007
1984 NCAA
NATIONAL CHAMPIONS
32
on Center
HAWKS
87
KOCH
nsecutive free
FREE CHICK-FIL-A
DWICH!
ETIHAD
ETIHAD

1

THE ROWDY GYM CLASS

Gym teacher **James Naismith** struggled to control a particularly boisterous class during the winter of 1891. His attempts to get them to play indoor football, lacrosse and soccer all ended in failure thanks to his students' tendency for rough play. Desperate to keep his class under control, Naismith invented a brand-new game by nailing two peach baskets high on the wall and explained that points could only be scored through a skilful looped throw, not sheer power. Basketball proved immediately popular and gave birth to the NBA we know today – and it's all thanks to an unruly class and their canny teacher.

2

PIVOTAL POINT GUARDS

To an inexperienced observer, basketball players move around the court in a haphazard manner, with no particular design or plan. But offensive plays run through the team's point guard in a similar manner to the quarterback on an American football team. The primary job of the point guard is to act as a playmaker, facilitating scoring opportunities for his teammates. After an opponent scores, it's typically the point guard who dribbles the ball down the court to begin an attack. Sometimes, they'll slow the game and work through a predesigned play. Other times, they'll instigate a fast break to counter an opponent who's out of position.

The best point guards are always aware of the shot clock, game clock and the overall position of the game. Magic Johnson and **Steph Curry** are archetypes of the ideal point guard – fast, good ball handling skills, and above all, exceptional vision. Although point guards aren't generally seven-foot giants, some height and muscle is ideal – although Muggsy Bogues proved that stature is subordinate to skill. His ball handling skills were so good that he played 889 games between 1987 and 2001, despite being only five feet, three inches and the shortest player ever to appear in the NBA.

3

THE SHOT

Michael Jordan made the first of his many iconic playoff game-winners when he took a dramatic final shot from the foul line in Game 5 of the Eastern Conference First Round series against the Cleveland Cavaliers. After six lead changes in the final minute, the Cavaliers had a one-point lead when Jordan received an inbound pass. He launched the ball over Craig Ehlo's head, it sank into the basket, and Jordan jumped around in celebration as the buzzer went. The Shot, as Jordan's basket came to be known, had clinched a close series that the Chicago Bulls entered as underdogs.

Having won all six regular season meetings between the teams, the Cavaliers' strength in depth had them pegged as the favourites, but it went down to a decider thanks to three consecutive 40-point games from Jordan. Jordan's wild display of emotion after sealing the win wasn't broadcast on television at the time since the live feed focused on Bulls coach Doug Collins sprinting down the sideline to his team, but later footage caught the happy outburst in all its glory. Cavs fans would soon be sick of the sight of Jordan. In Game 4 of the 1993 Eastern Conference Semi-Finals, Jordan made another series-winning buzzer-beater against the Cavaliers on the same end of the court.

4

THE GREEK FREAK

Giannis Antetokounmpo won consecutive MVP awards in 2019 and 2020 as he transformed his Milwaukee Bucks from also-rans into championship contenders. The following year, he slipped to fourth in the MVP voting, but more than made up for it with an NBA Championship ring – the Bucks' first title since 1971. Born in Greece to Nigerian parents, Giannis roamed the streets of Athens to hawk watches and handbags to tourists to help feed his family, and he was only recognised as a Greek citizen – giving him access to a passport – two months before the 2013 draft in which the Bucks selected him.

THE CHALK TOSS

As an NBA icon, all eyes are on **LeBron James** every time he takes to the court and eagle-eyed fans have noticed King James has an odd pre-game ritual. He walks to the side of the court, covers his hands in chalk, then throws some in the air before clapping. Some fans speculate it's done in honour of Michael Jordan, who once clapped chalk in the face of broadcaster Johnny Kerr. Others think it's a simple superstition. James himself claims that he can't remember how it started, but now can't stop since fans expect and enjoy his pre-game routine.

6 THE SCHEDULE FORMULA

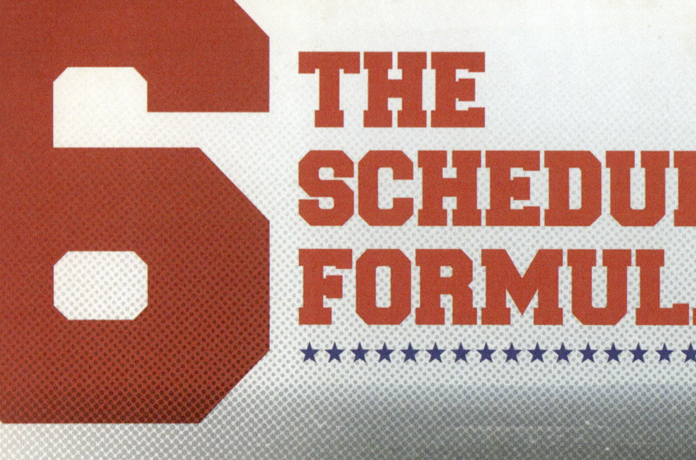

With 30 teams playing 82 games across six divisions in two conferences, NBA administrators face a real headache when they come to arrange each season's fixtures – a months-long process that involves a complicated algorithm with many variables being fed into a computer. Two priorities come into play: ensuring a fair and competitive schedule for every team, and keeping expenditure low by avoiding excessive travel. Each team plays four games against their other four division opponents, plus games against non-division opponents from the same conference, and a set number of games against every team in the opposing conference.

The addition of the In-Season Tournament has complicated matters even further, plus schedulers must take into consideration dates when a home team's court is unavailable due to pre-existing commitments. Ten teams share their home venue with NHL ice hockey franchises, many host concerts on off-days, while the **San Antonio Spurs** must vacate the Frost Bank Center for three weeks every February for an annual livestock show and rodeo. Given the complications that must be taken into account, it's no surprise that the NBA scheduling formula has featured as a case study in university research projects to illustrate mathematical concepts.

7

MR BASKETBALL

George Mikan was the NBA's first superstar. He came into the league during its second season with the Minneapolis Lakers and led his new team to five titles in six years from 1948. The lanky six-foot-ten-inch centre changed how teams used big men to play ball – Mikan towered over most of his opponents and used his height advantage to rebound, block and, more than anything else, shoot. Mikan led the NBA in scoring three times and was the first NBA player to breach 10,000 points. If there was a weakness in Mikan's game, it was that his long bones broke easily.

He suffered ten fractures throughout his career and pushed him into an early retirement – but by then, Mikan had already come to define the NBA's early years. He also faced one last battle. As one of the NBA's early stars, Mikan only earned a meagre wage. Despite being voted onto every NBA anniversary team, he was still only paid the $1700-a-month pension due to players who retired before 1965. Mikan died without an increase to his pension, but modern-day star Shaquille O'Neal paid for his funeral and talked passionately about Mikan's influence on the present day.

8

HEAD COACH HAMMON

The Women's NBA is one of the biggest and most successful women's sports leagues in the world, and the men's NBA embraced one of its best when the San Antonio Spurs appointed **Becky Hammon** as an assistant coach in 2014. She guided the team's Summer League in 2015, and in 2020, became the first woman to act as head coach when Spurs boss Gregg Popovich was ejected from the sideline for arguing with the officials. Hammon acted as a trailblazer for women in the NBA. In the six years after she got the job, another twelve women got coaching gigs with NBA teams.

OPENING NIGHT

The NBA season normally starts with a bang, with a short slate of games featuring high profile matchups including the defending champions in their home arena. Prior to tip-off, the previous season's title winners unveil the **championship banner** and players receive a memento of their success: their championships rings. Each season's ring is a bespoke design featuring the franchise's name, NBA logo, the year of the championship success and the player's name – making them immediately identifiable on the rare occasions a ring is sent to auction. Kareem Abdul-Jabbar gained $2.8 million for his charitable foundation by selling four NBA rings and other memorabilia in 2023.

9

10

CELEB SUPERFANS

Celebrities love to hog the limelight, and sitting in a prominent courtside position during a basketball game is an almost guaranteed way to get TV time. Although many A- to D-listers are there for the free publicity and social media moments, some celebs are genuine superfans. Spike Lee is an avid follower of the New York Knicks, even though his team hasn't enjoyed much success. He's butted heads with team management when he's been overzealous in his criticism of the franchise, and when the Knicks owner withdrew his complimentary tickets, he carried on spending more than $300,000 a year to attend games. Eminem is a die-hard Detroit Pistons fan, fellow rapper Drake follows the Toronto Raptors. **Jay-Z** was so into the Brooklyn Nets that bought a stake in the team.

He has also brought his wife **Beyoncé** to Nets games, but given she's a Houston native, she's more of a Rockets fan. But given its proximity to Hollywood, it's no surprise that the Los Angeles Lakers have the most A-listers on its courtside. Jack Nicholson has held a season ticket since 1970 and has witnessed the iconic exploits of Magic, Shaq, Kobe and LeBron in purple and gold.

11

MALICE AT THE PALACE

Although Game 8 of the 2004 regular season matchup between the Indiana Pacers and Detroit Pistons brought together the two teams who contested the previous year's Eastern Conference Finals, there wasn't a huge amount riding on this particular matchup. Nevertheless, it all kicked off with 45.9 seconds remaining in the fourth quarter. Pacers small forward **Ron Artest** fouled Pistons centre Ben Wallace in the back of the head as the latter went up for a lay-up, and Wallace retaliated by pushing Artest in the face.

It cleared the benches of both teams, but the officials regained control and things seemed to be calming down until Artest was hit by a drink thrown from by a fan. Artest jumped into the stands, punched a bystander who hadn't thrown the drink, and chaos descended on the arena again. Several fans invaded the court to attack players, some of whom responded with full-blown counterpunches. Other players joined the scuffles in the stands and the game was abandoned with the final 45 seconds unplayed. Artest was suspended for the rest of the season and faced criminal charges for assault, while several other players joined him on the sidelines for a prolonged period thanks to their roles in the unsavoury incident.

12

THE BIG FUNDAMENTAL

While many of the greatest players in history had flashy go-to moves, **Tim Duncan** had a distinctly understated approach. His celebrations were rarely animated, and he approached every game with a workmanlike mentality. However, there were few more competitive players on court. Duncan built a dynasty in 21st-century San Antonio with his super-consistent, never-back-down style of play. He won five titles and two MVP awards between 1999 and 2014. Every one of Duncan's 1,392 games came in a Spurs vest, and he finished his career high on the all-time lists for points, rebounds and blocks.

THE SALARY CAP

★★★★★★★★★★★★★★★★★★★★★★

Unlike the pro football and ice hockey leagues, basketball franchises don't have a fixed salary cap. Teams have a supposed ceiling beyond which they shouldn't spend, typically more than $125 million. Some choose to breach it, but if they do, they must pay a luxury tax on every dollar above the cap. They're also punished through restrictions on the contracts they can offer to free agents. The regulations ensure parity within the league and prevent a **big-money** team like the $6 billion Warriors, Lakers and Knicks from dominating purely due to the size of their bank balances.

13

14

THREE-POINTERS

On 12 October 1979, the Boston Celtics marked two momentous moments in NBA history. A young Larry Bird made his debut, beginning his journey to become a Celtics legend, but that went almost unnoticed thanks to a single **Chris Ford** shot. With less than four minutes remaining in the first quarter, Ford shot from distance to make the first three-pointer in an NBA game. The NBA was a late adopter of the three-point line. The American Basketball Association had it as early as 1967, but when the two pro leagues merged in 1976, the ABA teams didn't bring the three-pointer with them.

When it was introduced in the NBA, just in time for Larry Bird and Magic Johnson's rookie seasons, coaches had to adapt to the new normal. Some only chased three-pointers in the fourth quarter when their team was behind, but others designed offensive plays specifically to give their shooters the option of big points. No player has perfected the art of the long shot more than Steph Curry, who's made more than 3,500 three-pointers – not far off four a game with around a 40 per cent success rate. Curry's Golden State Warriors made a strategy of deep-ball plays, and it carried them to three championships in the 2010s.

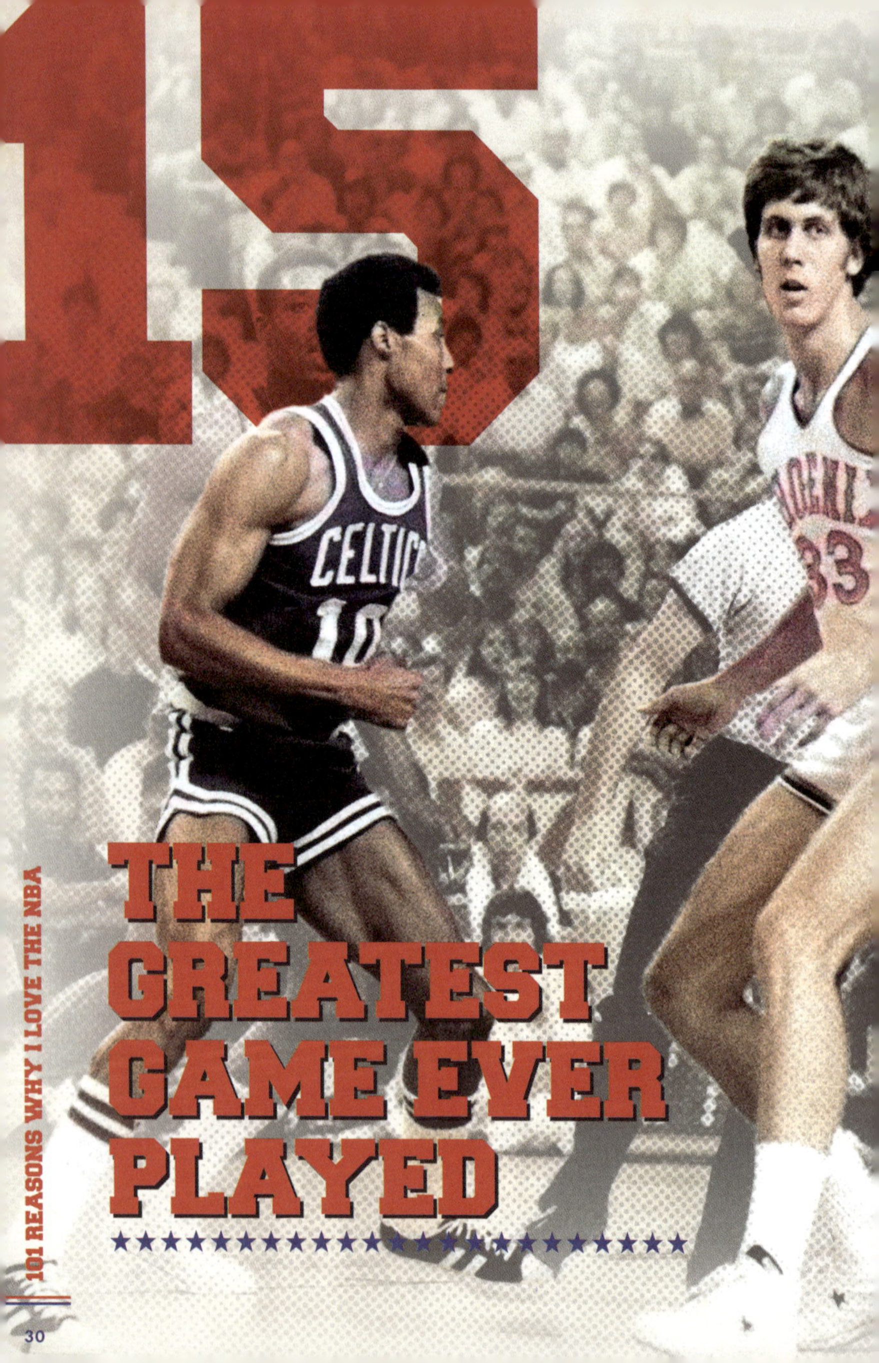

15

THE GREATEST GAME EVER PLAYED

The Phoenix Suns and **Boston Celtics** split the first four games in the 1976 NBA Finals, the last of which was an exciting see-saw game that went to overtime before the Suns won by two points. The fifth game, however, dwarfed the combined drama of everything that had happened so far. The teams couldn't be separated in regulation and first overtime. In the last 20 seconds of second overtime, the Celtics lost a three-point lead by conceding two quick baskets, then regained the lead with a basket by John Havlicek.

The Celtics seemed to have won the game and their fans invaded the court, only for the officials to rule that there were two seconds left to play. At the end of the second overtime, Suns player Paul Westphal intentionally called a timeout that his team didn't have, sacrificing a free-throw point to get possession of the ball at half-court. Gar Heard then made a buzzer-beater for the Suns to tie the game at 112-112. The Celtics finally eked out a win in the third OT, scoring 16 points to the Suns' 14 in the deciding five minutes, and the Greatest Game Ever Played was finally over.

16

SHAQ ATTACK

Shaquille O'Neal was an instant All-Star in Orlando playing for the Magic, but his pursuit of glory led him to sign with the Los Angeles Lakers in 1996, where teamed up with Kobe Bryant and won three straight titles in 2000, 2001 and 2002. O'Neal was named Finals MVP all three years, adding to his 2000 regular season MVP award. He moved on to pastures new several times in his later career and added a fourth title with the Miami Heat in 2006. O'Neal's career player efficiency rating (PER) of 26.4 ranks third all-time, behind only Michael Jordan and LeBron James.

MASCOTS

★★★★★★★★★★★★

Forget the iconic stars of the NBA – when it comes to the league's youngest fans, it's all about the crazily dressed team mascots. Despite their massive and unwieldy costumes, many of these colourful characters can dance, perform and even slam dunk. Many mascots make it their full-time job, attending community and charity events as a rep of the team. Rocky the Mountain Lion (Denver Nuggets), **Harry the Hawk** (Atlanta Hawks) and Benny the Bull (Chicago Bulls) are among the NBA's most popular mascots, but the Lakers, Nets, Knicks and Warriors' courts are sadly lacking when it comes to a furry friend.

17

18

DYNASTIES

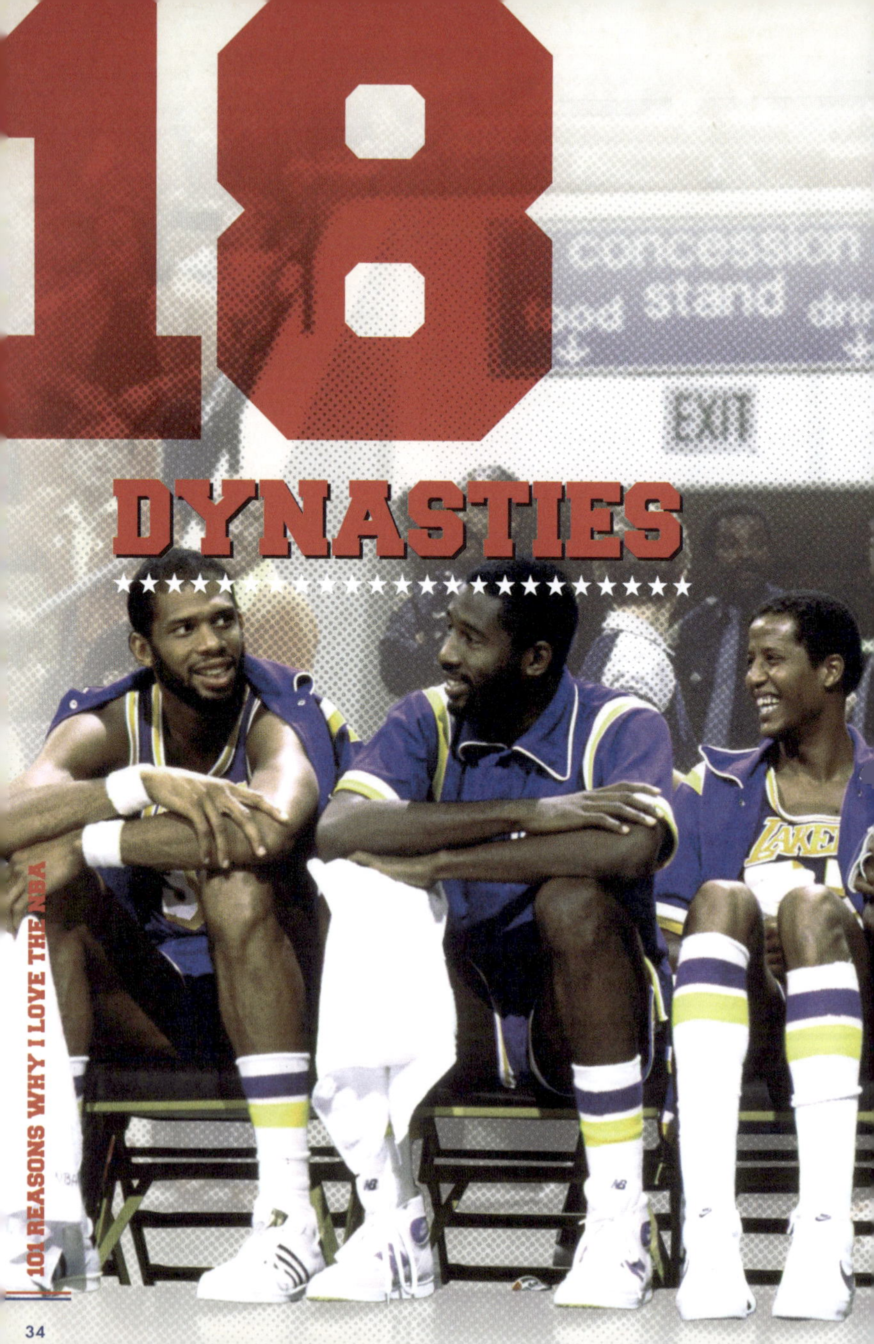

Although the salary cap and draft are designed to ensure that no single team rules the NBA, there have been occasions when one team has gained multiple titles over a short period of time. The first of these dynasties, as American sports fans like to call them, was the Boston Celtics. They won 11 titles in 13 years, including eight in a row, between 1957 and 1969. But all good things (for Bostonians at least) must come to an end, and the 1970s ushered in a more egalitarian era. Every decade since has tended to be enjoyed by one team more than the others.

The 'Showtime' Los Angeles Lakers were the team of the 1980s thanks to Magic Johnson and Kareem Abdul-Jabbar. They had five titles in nine seasons and were runners-up a couple more times. The Chicago Bulls had two three-peats in the 1990s, and the **Los Angeles Lakers** had their own hat-trick of titles when the new millennium dawned. Most recently, the Golden State Warriors were the team to beat after 2015. They had five consecutive NBA Finals appearances, coming away with three championship rings, and an extra NBA title three years after that.

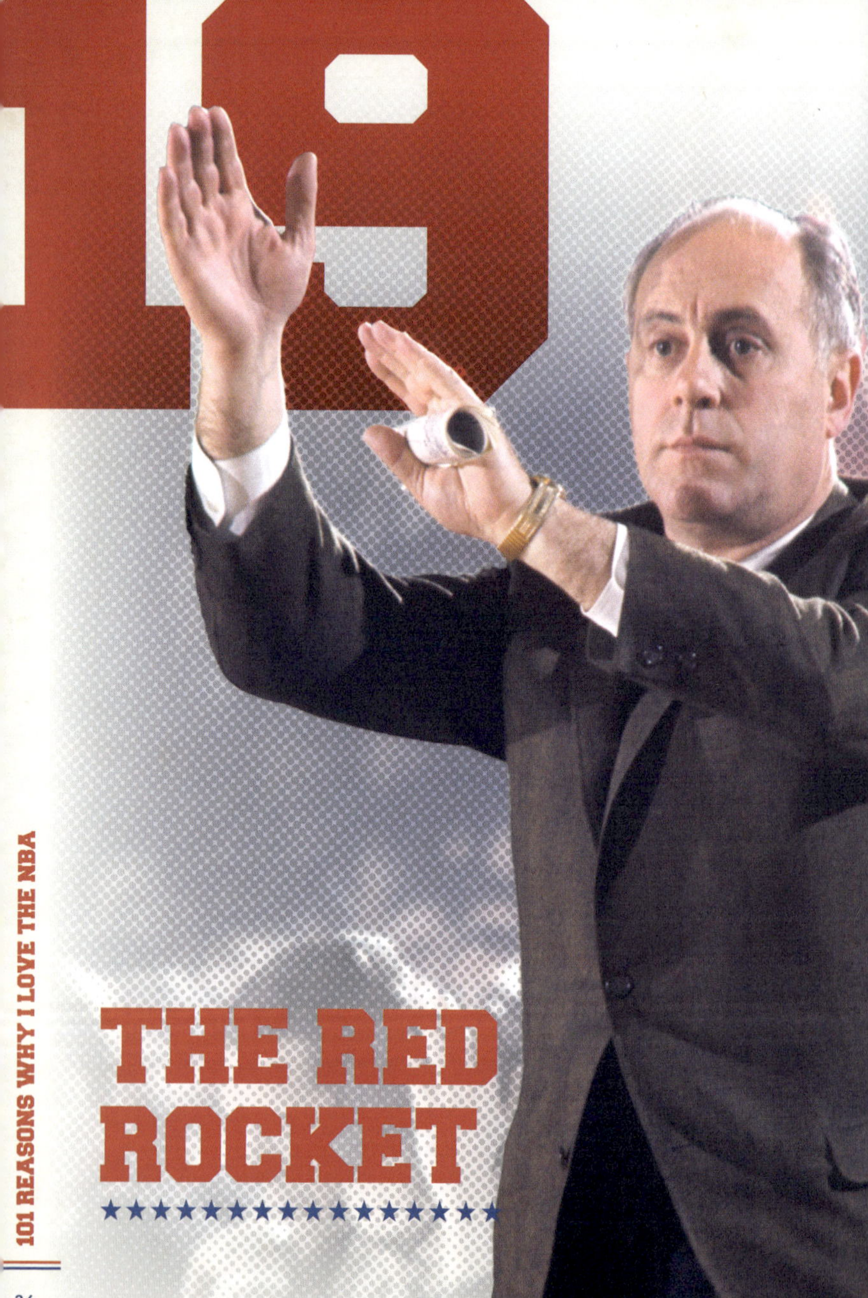

THE RED ROCKET

Orchestrating a trade for Bill Russell after the 1956 NBA draft would have been enough to enshrine **Arnold 'Red' Auerbach** in Boston Celtics lore – Russell is possibly the greatest defensive player in league history – but Auerbach then proceeded to build a multi-title-winning roster around his defensive giant in an era when offensive statistics were a shorthand for a team and coach's success. Auerbach is credited as a key innovator in the fast break offense, which stressed moving the ball before the opposing defence had time to organise properly, but he has a greater legacy than leading his Celtics to nine NBA titles.

Auerbach was also a pioneer of racial integration: the first coach to draft a Black player and the first to adopt an entirely Black starting line-up. The Coach of the Year trophy is named after him, and no fewer than 30 of the players Auerbach coached went on to have their own coaching careers. Auerbach's final foray into coaching came in 1984, when he took charge of a veterans' team at the All-Star Game. Age had not dimmed his competitive spirit, and he was ejected for arguing with the officials.

20

THE 50-POINT CLINCHER

★★★★★★★★★★★★

26-year-old **Giannis Antetokounmpo** was a doubt for the 2021 NBA Finals after suffering a nasty knee injury during the Eastern Conference finals, but he was cleared to play by team medics and went on to put in a career-defining performance. Antetokounmpo was named Finals MVP after almost single-handedly dragging the Milwaukee Bucks back into the series from 2-0 down. He clinched the Bucks' first championship title in 50 years with 50 points in Game 6 – equalling the top score by a single player in a Finals decider – thanks to a staggering improvement in his free-throw percentage.

VERSATILE SMALL FORWARDS

★★★★★★★★★★★★★★★★★★★★★★★★

Don't be misled by the name – short forwards in the NBA average between six-feet, six-inches and six-feet, nine-inches. Their job is to score points, although exactly how they do that varies widely. Some like to attack at speed and slash into from the wings, others like to dominate near the basket. The latter technique helped LeBron James become the highest-scoring player in NBA history, while **Kevin Durant** relies on shot accuracy. On defence, small forwards are required to guard multiple positions – but, as in attack, different small forwards employ different tactics to stop their opponents.

21

22

WNBA

In 1996, the NBA approved the creation of a new women's league that carried its full backing. The Women's NBA, or WNBA, carries a similar logo to the men's game and several teams share arenas with their male counterparts. The league began amid great publicity thanks to the US women's team winning gold at the 1996 Olympics, and the new WNBA franchises scrambled to sign the gold medallists. The Houston Comets won the race for Team USA lynchpin **Sheryl Swoopes**, and she became the first player to sign a WNBA contract.

Swoopes was a late debutant thanks to pregnancy, but when she finally did take to the court, she quickly became the poster girl for the new pro league. She amassed over 2,000 points, won four titles with the Comets, and was named MVP on three occasions. Since then, Diana Taurasi, Tamika Catchings and Sue Bird have helped elevate the WNBA to a new level. It was the first pro sports league to launch a Pride campaign to back the LGBTQ community and the first to respond to the Black Lives Matter protests, and game attendance and television viewership figures are on the up as fans take renewed interest in the women's game.

AIR JORDAN

Although LeBron James has his champions, most basketball fans think there's only one name under consideration as the GOAT: the Greatest of All Time. **Michael Jordan** was instantly heralded as the Chicago Bulls' lynchpin when he was drafted by the team in 1984, but he didn't win his first NBA title until his seventh season in the league. Yet once he had that first ring, no one else stood a chance. Topping the league in scoring seven years in a row, Jordan led the Bulls to three titles on the trot.

He quit the Bulls to try his hand at baseball, but his supposed retirement turned out to be an 18-month sabbatical. Jordan assumed complete control of the NBA once again the next season, leading the Bulls to another three straight titles while nabbing another three scoring titles. He promptly retired again, unretired again, and enjoyed two more seasons with the Washington Wizards before calling time for good at 39 years old and five MVP awards in his trophy cabinet. No active player seems likely to beat his 30.1 points-per-game career average, and had he not taken two periods out of the game, Jordan would be higher than fifth place on the all-time points list.

THE DAWKINS DUNKS

★★★★★★★★★★★★★★★★★★

Darryl Dawkins, the self-proclaimed Chocolate Thunder, was known for his brutal dunks. In November 1979, he dunked so hard that the backboard shattered, raining glass onto the defender who'd vainly tried to block him. Three weeks later, he did the same thing. Though he wasn't the first backboard-breaker, Dawkins' antics persuaded the NBA to invest in breakaway rings with springs that allowed them to bend and snap back into position without breaking. Even so, Shaquille O'Neal's monster dunks still managed to break the supports holding the backboard twice in the 1992-93 season, leading to extra steel braces being mandated.

GLOBAL GAMES

NBA teams have played occasional exhibitions against foreign opposition since the Washington Bullets lost to Maccabi Tel Aviv in Israel in 1978. Since then, the NBA has sent teams abroad for both exhibition and regular season matchups. In recent years, **Mexico City** has been a favourite destination, with additional matches in Paris and London. The aim of the Global Games is to increase the NBA's presence in these foreign markets. At a time when basketball is already one of the most popular sports in the United States, the best opportunities for growth come beyond the country's borders.

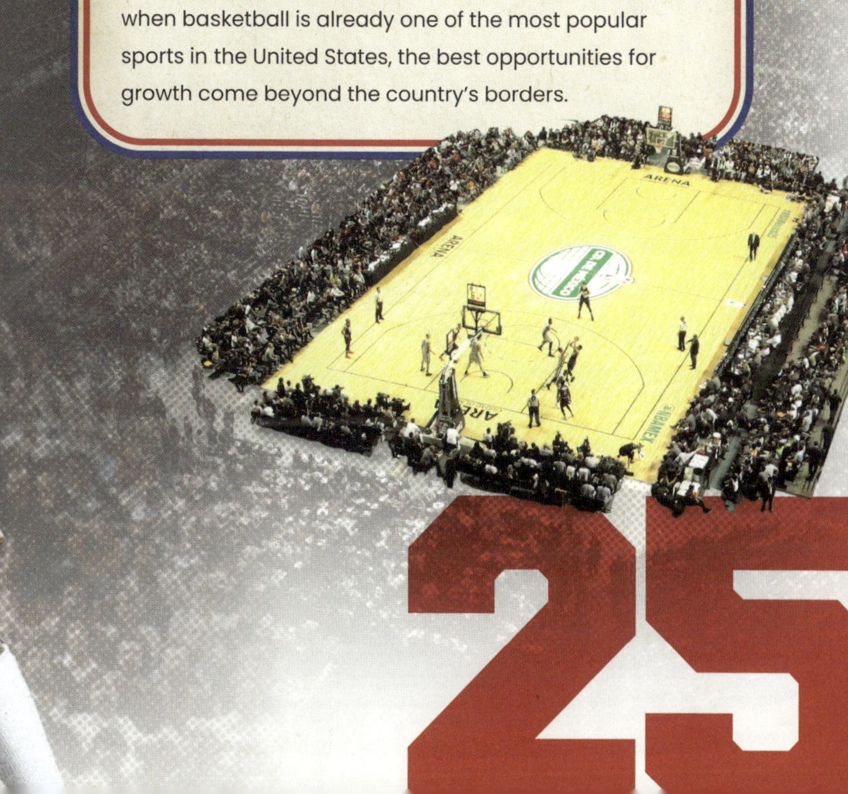

25

26

THE SIXTH MAN

While the five starters are the headliners, the sixth man is the support act – but they're still a crucial part of the roster. They come off the bench, often the first to be substituted in, and play more minutes than the other bench players – sometimes the starters too. The most valuable sixth men play multiple positions to enable a coach to alter the course of the game. Some are good shooters to keep the scoreboard ticking over when the starters swap out, others are playmakers who spend the first quarter watching and identifying an opponent's weaknesses.

The sixth-man strategy was pioneered by Boston Celtics coach Red Auerbach. He used guard Frank Ramsey as an off-the-bench player to swap in for Bob Cousy and Bill Sharman. A few seasons later, John Havlicek took over the role. Both Ramsey and Havlicek could easily have become starters on other rosters, but Auerbach convinced them of their importance in Boston. In 1983, the NBA recognised the impact of sixth men with a new award. Since then, Jamal Crawford and **Lou Williams** have won it three times, more than any other player, and Williams is the NBA career leader for both points and games off the bench.

27

THE BIG SCORE

The 21st-century NBA might be a high-scoring league, but it's got nothing on the 1980s. The four biggest scores in NBA history all took place during that decade, and remarkably, three of them occurred at McNichols Arena in Denver. The Nuggets didn't have a particularly complex playbook. Instead, head coach Doug Moe asked his players to run fast and run long, and the quick offense led to some fast scoring. Never was that more the case than in December 1983, when the **Denver Nuggets** took on the equally nippy **Detroit Pistons**.

Together, they put up 370 points in a triple-overtime game. It featured 142 field goals (only two of which were three-pointers) and 93 assists. Four players scored at least 40 points, led by Kiki VanDeWeghe's 51 for Denver – he'd never score more in the rest of his career. Alex English added 47 points for the Denver Nuggets, while Isiah Thomas equalled that number for Detroit, and John Long scored 41. It eventually came to an end with a successful Thomas free throw – the 117th free-throw attempt of the game – that made the score 186-184 to the Pistons. No doubt the players were tired, but the scoreboard operators must have been ready to collapse.

28

THE MAILMAN

★★★★★★★★★★★★★

The player who always delivered, **Karl Malone** appeared in 1,476 games over his 19 years in the NBA, all bar one for the Utah Jazz. A two-time MVP, Malone ended his career with 36,928 points and the all-time free-throw leader with 9,787. His final season came with the Los Angeles Lakers at the age of 40 in one last, unsuccessful effort to gain the NBA ring that had eluded him. Even though his team never won the NBA title, the 14-time All-Star is remembered as one of the greatest power forwards to take to the court.

G LEAGUE

★★★★★★★★★★★★★

The NBA doesn't just run the pro league we all know and love, it also oversees a minor league to develop upcoming players. The **G League** is run slightly differently to its bigger brother. Some players are signed to NBA contracts and sent to the G League to gain experience. Others went unselected in the main NBA Draft but are considered to have potential as big-league players. These players go into a second-chance G League Draft and those chosen are employed directly by the G League, creating a pool of players who can be called up by any NBA franchise that requires their services.

30

SNEAKERS

Basketball and sneakers go hand-in-hand – or should that be foot-in-shoe? Footwear is one of the few areas that players have any real power to choose their own equipment, and specialist gear goes back to 1921, when semi-pro player Chuck Taylor began working for Converse as a salesman and design consultant. For decades since, **Converse** was the shoe of choice for the majority of players. By the 1980s, shoe manufacturers began to sign big-name players to endorsement deals, paying them megabucks for the privilege of supplying them with free footwear.

Converse still had the most players, including Larry Bird and Magic Johnson, but Adidas had wooed Kareem Abdul-Jabbar with the promise of a signature line in his name. The sneaker market went stratospheric when a lesser-known manufacturer signed an up-and-coming star from the 1984 Draft. Nike's partnership with Michael Jordan unleashed the **Air Jordan**. Thanks to an innovative marketing campaign and Jordan's instant impact on the NBA, Air Jordans became a cultural phenomenon, creating long lines at retailers. Air Jordans are still going strong today, having earned billions for Nike and the player the brand is based around, and every other manufacturer has tried to copy their success with varying degrees of success.

31

THE MERGER

The NBA hasn't always had things its own way. In 1967, the American Basketball Association (ABA) was formed as a rival pro league, and its owners were happy to engage in a bidding war for top talent. The Milwaukee Bucks of the NBA did manage to secure the best college star of the era – a centre then known as Lew Alcindor, soon to become Kareem Abdul-Jabbar – but the NBA's reigning top scorer, Rick Barry, jumped ship. He withdrew from his contract with the San Francisco Warriors to sign with the Oakland Oaks of the ABA. Four veteran referees were also tempted by the better pay offered by the rival league.

The NBA tried to outmuscle the ABA by expanding into parts of the country that had no pro basketball. Soon, the Buffalo Braves, Cleveland Cavaliers, New Orleans Jazz and Portland Trail Blazers joined the league. Ultimately, co-operation rather than competition was the best way to end basketball's civil war, and in 1976, the NBA agreed to assimilate the ABA. As part of the deal, four out of ten ABA teams joined the NBA: the Denver Nuggets, **Indiana Pacers**, **New York Nets** and San Antonio Spurs. It also brought the ABA's standout player, Julius Erving, into the NBA fold.

32

THE BIG DIPPER

Wilt Chamberlain's NBA career saw him gain two championship rings. It would have been more had he not come up against fellow Hall of Fame centre Bill Russell so often in the playoffs. During Chamberlain's 15 years in Philadelphia, San Francisco and Los Angeles, he set NBA records that will probably never be broken: among them a single-season average of 50.4 points and 25.7 rebounds per game set in 1961-62. Chamberlain is the only NBA player to score 100 points in a game, and only Michael Jordan has averaged more than Chamberlain's 30.1 career points-per-game.

ASSISTS

★★★★★★★★★★★

Most of the glory goes to the players who score the baskets, especially if they do so with a spectacular slam dunk or shot from distance, but coaches also count assists – the pass that leads to a scoring shot – as a key statistical category. Most assists go to point guards as the playmakers of the team, though some centres excel in creating opportunities for others. Nobody did it better than **John Stockton**, who amassed more than 15,000 career assists with the Utah Jazz, though the single-game record is held by Scott Skiles, who had 30 in one game for the Orlando Magic in 1990.

34 THE DRAFT LOTTERY

As in most North American pro sports, the NBA gives the worst teams from the previous season the chance to pick the best college prospects in an annual draft. Giving the first choice to the lowest-performing teams helps to keep parity within the league, with every team knowing a hot new star might lift them from worst to first. But the traditional draft system is open to teams playing the system and tanking – deliberately losing to snaffle a player identified as a generational talent.

To prevent this, the top four picks in the NBA Draft are decided by a **lottery**. The 14 teams who miss out on the playoffs go into a random draw, with varying chances of success depending on their win-loss record. The three teams with the worst record have a 14% chance of their name being called. After the first four picks are decided by the draft, the order of picks five and onwards revert to the usual regular-season record system. Not everybody thinks the draft lottery is perfect, and some would like to alter the weightings and the process, but it does ensure that lower-performing teams have a fair opportunity to improve.

35

KING JAMES

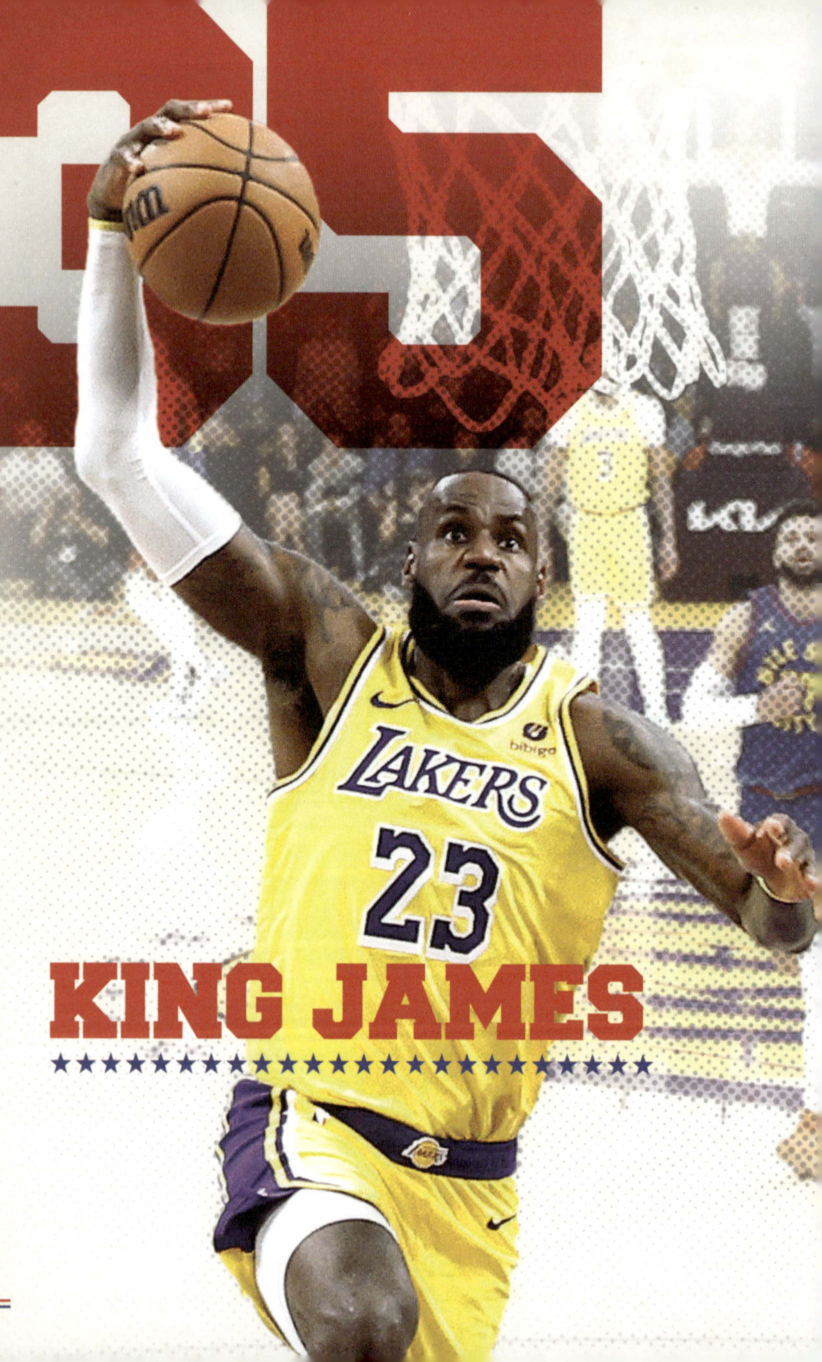

★★★★★★★★★★★★★★★★★★★★★★★★

Undoubtedly the best player of the 21st century, and perhaps the only contender to knock Michael Jordan off his throne as the GOAT, **LeBron James** has dominated the NBA since he was drafted by the Cleveland Cavaliers amid huge hype in 2003. He soon matched the sky-high expectations, being named Rookie of the Year in 2004 and NBA MVP in 2009 and 2010 thanks to his high-scoring and versatile skillset. James won two consecutive NBA titles with the Miami Heat in 2012 and 2013 before returning to Cleveland and leading the Cavs to their first-ever title in 2016.

He won a fourth ring with the Los Angeles Lakers in 2020 and broke Kareem Abdul-Jabbar's all-time scoring record in 2023. James has had a huge influence on modern basketball and has come to symbolise an increase in player power. He's shown a willingness to switch teams during free agency in his quest to be a part of the best roster while being paid handsomely for his services. Thanks to this mercenary approach, James was the first active NBA player to become a billionaire thanks to a reported $430 million in salary and more than $900 million in endorsements.

36

THE BABY HOOK

★★★★★★★

Magic Johnson was enjoying his first MVP season in 1987 when the Los Angeles Lakers met the Boston Celtics in the NBA Finals, and Game 3 went down to the wire. After Kareem Abdul-Jabbar missed a free throw to tie the game, Johnson got the ball on the baseline with seven seconds to go. Rather than dump-off the ball to Jabbar for a slam dunk, Johnson ran parallel to the backline and launched a mini skyhook, arcing the ball in a wide one-handed throw to keep it away from the Celtics defenders to hit a spectacular game-winning basket.

OUTDOOR GAMES

Basketball is primarily an indoor sport at pro level since the NBA wants games to be decided by the best players rather than the vagaries of wind and rain, but four games have bucked the trend, all involving the **Phoenix Suns**. They played a preseason game against the Milwaukee Bucks on an outdoor court in Puerto Rico in 1972, then preseason encounters at the Indian Wells tennis complex in 2008, 2009 and 2010. Thankfully, none of the games were played in the torrential rain that spoiled the first ever Olympic basketball final in Berlin in 1936.

37

38

HALL OF FAME

★★★★★★★★★★★★★★★★★★★★★★★★★★★

More than 4,000 men have played in the NBA since it was created in 1946 – but less than 200 have been deemed worthy of inclusion in the Naismith Memorial **Hall of Fame**. This institution, based in Springfield, Massachusetts, is named after James Naismith, the gym teacher who invented the sport at one of the city's colleges. Naismith was one of the inaugural class of inductees in 1959 and was classified as a 'contributor'. Joining him in that category over the years have been NBA commissioners, team owners, administrators and broadcasters.

Around 100 individuals are in the Hall of Fame as coaches, and less than 20 are referees. But each year, most attention is given to the new cohort of players chosen. Six committees screen potential names, each with a specialist interest: women's basketball, early Black players, veterans, international basketball, and the most prestigious panel that supervises the recent NBA. After these committees prepare shortlists of potential inductees, the final say goes to the 24-person Honors Committee. Over the years, they've approved such luminaries as Jerry West (1980), Larry Bird (1998) and Kobe Bryant, who was elected posthumously, a few months after his death in a helicopter crash in 2020.

39

THE ZEN MASTER

★★★★★★★★★★★★★★★★

Critics of **Phil Jackson** think that the teams he coached won 11 NBA titles only because he had stellar players at his disposal. Yes, Jackson benefited from rosters featuring Michael Jordan, Shaquille O'Neal and Kobe Bryant, but nobody picks up an unrivalled 1,155 regular season wins at a 70.4 win percentage – and 229 playoff victories at an almost-as-impressive 68.8 per cent – through luck alone. In an era where player power and egos were growing, Jackson kept his superstar rosters functioning smoothly. Six NBA titles in seven seasons is an amazing accomplishment, but Jackson not only accomplished that from 1996 to 2002, but he split them equally across two different teams: the Chicago Bulls and Los Angeles Lakers.

Jackson was a pioneer of the triangle offense, and he had one of the system's key innovators, Tex Winter, on his staff with both the Bulls and the Lakers. That offensive scheme was key in the development of Jordan, who had been targeted by opposing defences prior to its installation in 1989. Jackson employed unconventional methods dreamed up while he read philosophy, and among the many quotes attributed to him, Jackson uttered: 'Good teams become great ones when the members trust each other enough to surrender the Me for the We.'

40

THE BUZZER BEATER

The Toronto Raptors and Philadelphia 76ers were tied at 90 apiece in the final game of the Eastern Conference Semi-Final series in 2019 and the game seemed destined for overtime when Raptors forward **Kawhi Leonard** got the ball with seconds to go. In a last effort to end the game, he hit a shot from the corner over Joel Embiid. The buzzer sounded when the ball was in the air, and the ball bounced off the rim four times before it finally fell into the basket to provoke rapturous celebrations. It was the first buzzer-beater to win a deciding Game 7 in NBA history.

CHRISTMAS GAMES

For basketball fans, Christmas means holidays, holly and hoops. The NBA has held fixtures on **Christmas Day** since 1947 when the New York Knicks hosted the Providence Steamrollers, and five games are now usually held on the big day. There are no fixed teams or venues involved. Instead, the league chooses some big matchups to take advantage of relatively free television schedules, since NHL and NFL tend not to play on Christmas Day. Often, the previous year's playoff teams are involved, or two teams with well-known rivalries are showcased – and the season of goodwill doesn't always extend to the court.

SKYSCRAPER CENTRES

It's difficult to miss the centre – they're usually the tallest player on the team, close to seven feet in height. Thanks to their stature, centres are valued for their ability to defend their own basket and grab rebounds on offense. Few did it better than Bill Russell and Wilt Chamberlain, the Boston Celtics and Philadelphia 76ers centres who duelled throughout the 1960s. The introduction of the three-point line saw the importance of the centre recede, although big men are still a valuable part of the team.

The Washington Bullets tried to pioneer a new defence-first approach to centre play when they drafted the tallest players in NBA history – **Manute Bol** and Gheorghe Muresan were both listed as seven-foot seven-inch beanpoles when they were drafted in 1985 and 1993, and Bol is the only player with more shots blocked than points scored during his career. But rather than double-down on defensive centres, most teams decided to adapt their centre strategy and focus on offense instead. A new generation of Eastern European centres like Vlade Divac and Arvydas Sabonis proved that centres could operate successfully on the perimeter, a tradition that Nikola Jokic is keeping alive with the Denver Nuggets.

43

Abbotts
Pasteurized
Homogenized
Modified
Vitamin D Milk
PHIL
13

WILT'S 100

★★★★★★★★★★★★★★★★★★★★★

On 2 March 1962, **Wilt Chamberlain** set an NBA record that's as iconic to basketball fans as Roger Bannister's four-minute mile is to runners. As the Philadelphia Warriors cruised to a 169-147 victory over the New York Knicks, Chamberlain just kept scoring, and scoring, and scoring. At the end of the game, he had a nice, round 100 points – the only time an NBA player has hit three figures in a single game. It was a free-flowing contest – the combined points total of 316 was an NBA record at the time – and with Knicks centre Phil Jordan sidelined by the flu, Chamberlain could not be contained by stand-ins Darrall Imhoff and Cleveland Buckner. He scored 23 points in the first quarter, 41 in the second and 28 in the third.

By the fourth, sensing that something special was happening, fans began to chant Chamberlain's name. The Warriors continued to feed him the ball at every opportunity while the Knicks desperately tried to block him. Finally, Chamberlain took a pass from Joe Ruklick and hit a short shot with 46 seconds left to give him 100 points. It obliterated the previous single-game record of 78 points – a mark set by Chamberlain three months earlier – and remains unlikely to be broken anytime soon.

44

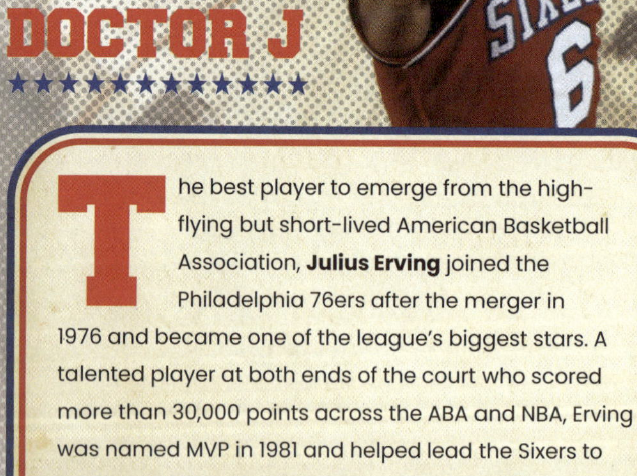

DOCTOR J

The best player to emerge from the high-flying but short-lived American Basketball Association, **Julius Erving** joined the Philadelphia 76ers after the merger in 1976 and became one of the league's biggest stars. A talented player at both ends of the court who scored more than 30,000 points across the ABA and NBA, Erving was named MVP in 1981 and helped lead the Sixers to the title in 1983. His signature move was the slam dunk, a move that he brought into the mainstream and transformed from a simple show of force into a high-percentage way to finish off an offensive play.

TRADE DEADLINE

Throughout the year, NBA general managers fine-tune their rosters by doing deals with other GMs. Sometimes, a simple like-for-like swap gives underachieving players a second chance under a fresh coaching structure. More often, a team in search of a particular type of talent offers a battery of players, cash and draft picks to get the player they want. The dealing reaches a crescendo at the **trade deadline** near the All-Star break, when teams in playoff contention try to get an extra boost while slumping teams aim to offload high-salary players in anticipation of an offseason rebuild.

46

OFF THE BOARDS

Missed shots cause a free-for-all on the basketball court as players from both teams fight to take control of the ball. Defenders tend to be in a better position to snaffle the ball, but if an attacker can grab it, their team gets a second bite of the cherry. Perhaps that's why rebounds are considered one of the key statistical measures of a player's worth.

Great rebounders tend to be tall and strong because they can reach the ball over the outstretched hands of their opponents, but a lack of height can be compensated for by strength to box out an opponent – positioning themselves between the basket and an opponent and not letting them through. Larry Bird, **Jason Kidd** and Moses Malone had good rebound rates despite lacking in height compared to their peers, while Charles Barkley was among the best despite being inches shorter than the typical power forward. Sometimes, all it takes is a little determination. Kenneth Faried once single-handedly bamboozled three defenders by grabbing four rebounds in ten seconds from his own shots. He tried again and again to get the ball in the basket, only succeeding on the fifth attempt.

47

THE BUBBLE

★★★★★★★★★★★★★★★★★★★★★★★

The world went into lockdown in March 2020 after the Covid-19 pandemic struck the globe, and the NBA was no exception. After a few weeks of enforced isolation, NBA bosses looked for an extraordinary way to end the season in extraordinary times. At the time the league was suspended, eight teams were already out of playoff contention. The remaining 22 teams were invited to compete in a bio-secure venue: Walt Disney World in Florida, which stood empty due to Covid-19 restrictions. With no travel, no spectators, and no players allowed to leave the NBA 'bubble', it was hoped that the season would finish without further outbreaks.

Teams arrived at Disney World by 21 July after a month of rigorous testing to ensure they were all clear of the virus, then played exhibitions to get them back to fitness. Eight regular season games finalised the seedings, then the usual playoff format was followed. It all ended with the **Los Angeles Lakers** winning another NBA title, but there was an even greater success: over the 93 days that the bubble was active, not a single case of Covid-19 was reported among NBA players and staff and the Disney employees who tended to them.

48

ZEKE

★★★★★★★

One of the greatest point guards of all time, **Isiah Thomas** spent his whole career with the Detroit Pistons and came to personify the Bad Boys as they battled with Michael Jordan's Chicago Bulls. The GOAT didn't always win – Thomas led the Pistons to back-to-back titles in 1989 and 1990, and Thomas was named Finals MVP in 1990. He was a tempestuous player who would back teammates to the max, and his opponents hated playing against him. Though barely over six feet, Thomas was a good scorer and an elite passer, and he still holds a host of franchise records.

CHEERLEADERS

NBA **cheerleaders** are mostly part-time professionals who spend hours learning routines and attending charity events and fundraisers on behalf of their team. They entertain the crowd before the game and during stoppages, though recent years have seen the pom-poms and skimpy outfits of all-female cheer squads dropped in favour of more family-friendly dance troupes and hype teams – and the San Antonio Spurs have got rid of theirs completely. Several former cheerleaders have gone on to careers in broadcasting and entertainment, none more successfully than a performer who was part of the Los Angeles Lakers cheer crew in the 1980s: Paula Abdul.

50
THE BENCHES
NBA
PHILA
StubHub

A quick glance at any courtside **bench** reveals that players who are waiting their turn sit alongside a host of support staff. The head coach is always there, as is the athletic trainer who deals with strains and injuries, but NBA rules also state that three assistant coaches can join them on the front row. Behind them, on the second row, other assistants are hard at work. It takes an entire coaching staff to put a team's strategy into effect. The lead assistant consults with the head coach to offer guidance and suggestions.

One assistant is likely to have taken the lead on scouting that night's opponents and watches the other team with an eagle eye, making play calls if he thinks he's cracked their system. The second-row assistants are likely tracking every play with a video coordinator, logging timestamps and marking up plays to be shown by the head coach at half-time. Others will be analysing offensive plays, defensive plays, another will be focusing on opposition plays. The assistants track every small detail in real time, allowing the head coach to look at the big picture and making game-time adjustments without getting bogged down in the data.

51

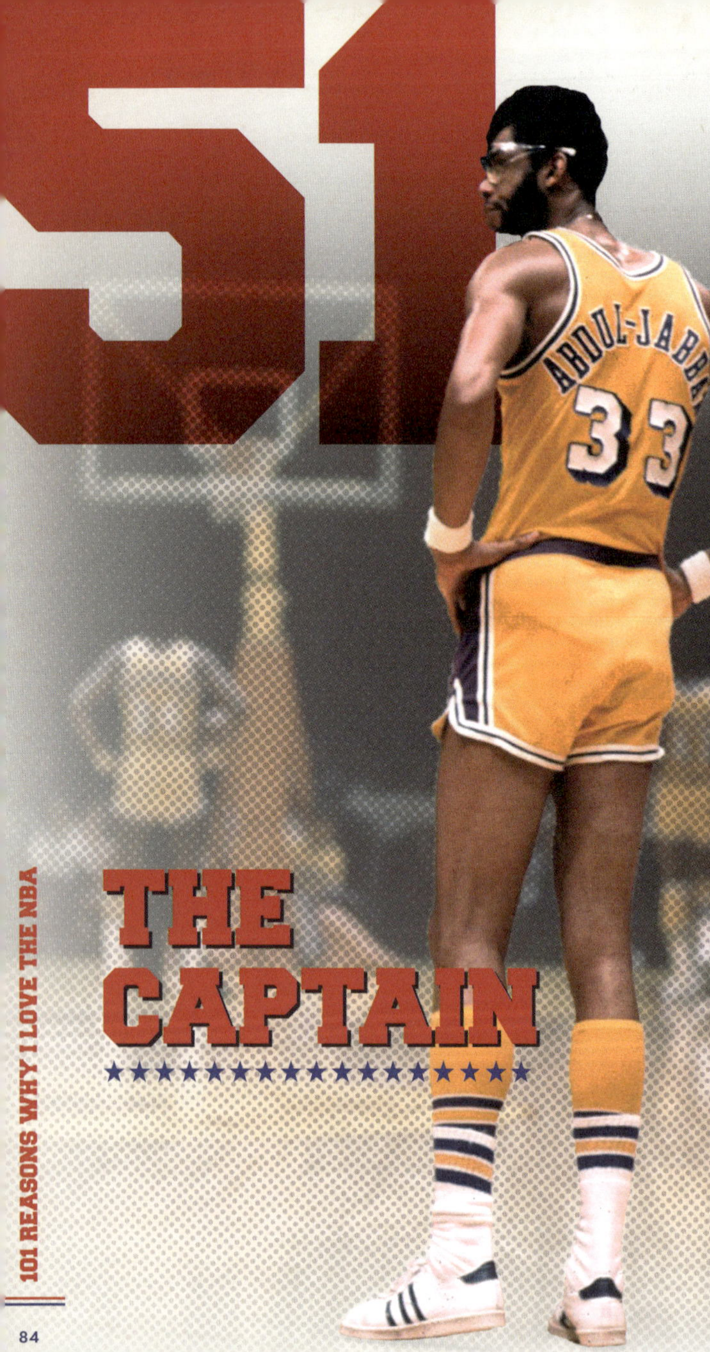

THE CAPTAIN

The player we now know as **Kareem Abdul-Jabbar** entered the league in 1969 as Lew Alcindor and changed his name after converting to Islam in 1971. That came a short time after he won his first NBA ring with the Milwaukee Bucks, and he gained a further five titles after moving to the Los Angeles Lakers in 1975. Jabbar was an inspiration both on and off the court. He was named MVP six times in a ten-year period between 1971 and 1980 and has 19 All-Star selections.

His signature move was the skyhook, a difficult one-handed jump shot in which he swept the ball round in a wide arc. Jabbar thought the longevity of his career was due to a combination of yoga and Eastern spirituality – he was certainly unusual in the care that he looked after his body, and that helped him to play all 82 games in five different seasons. At the time of his retirement after 20 years in the NBA, Jabbar was the league's top scorer as well as the record-holder for most games played and minutes played. He was also a fierce human rights campaigner, having realised the influence he could wield as a sporting celebrity and role model.

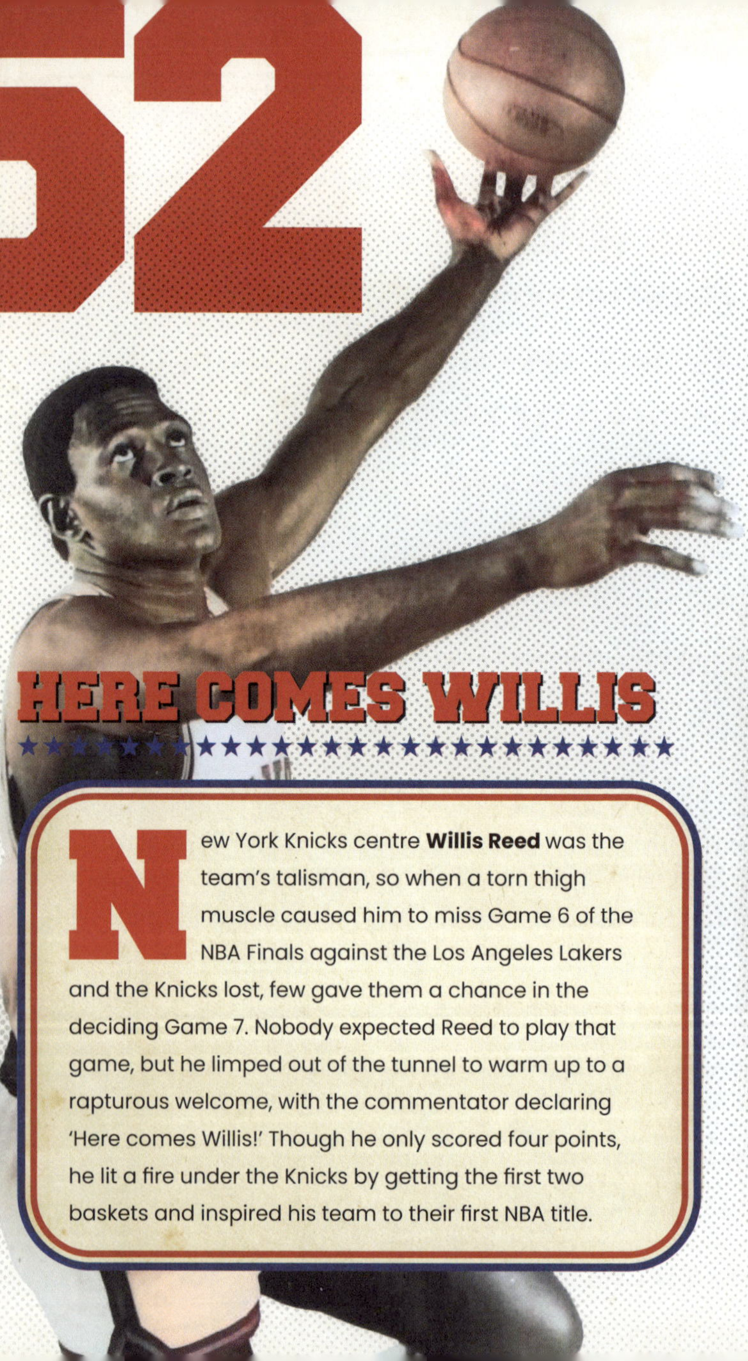

52

HERE COMES WILLIS

New York Knicks centre **Willis Reed** was the team's talisman, so when a torn thigh muscle caused him to miss Game 6 of the NBA Finals against the Los Angeles Lakers and the Knicks lost, few gave them a chance in the deciding Game 7. Nobody expected Reed to play that game, but he limped out of the tunnel to warm up to a rapturous welcome, with the commentator declaring 'Here comes Willis!' Though he only scored four points, he lit a fire under the Knicks by getting the first two baskets and inspired his team to their first NBA title.

ALLEY-OOP

French acrobats used to cry 'Allez hop!' before attempting a death-defying leap. Basketball players adopted an Americanised version of the phrase to describe one of their most acrobatic moves: passing the ball to a jumping teammate who catches and scores with a dunk or lay up before touching the ground. NBA stars make the spectacular play look easy, but it requires almost perfect timing and dexterity, and a natural chemistry between teammates – the kind of relationship that **DeAndre Jordan** had with **Chris Paul** for the Los Angeles Clippers, helping them to the best alley-oop the NBA has ever seen in 2013.

54

NBA ACADEMY

Although basketball is primarily seen as an American sport, talented athletes from all over the world have ambitions to play in the NBA. To give players from lesser-known basketball nations a pathway to the big league, the NBA has created **academies** in Australia, India, Mexico and Senegal to coach young prospects and give them the skillsets they need to succeed. Youngsters from around the globe are identified at another NBA program, Junior NBA, and offered placements at their nearest academy for coaching with education and housing also provided. Australian point guard Josh Giddey became the first NBA Academy graduate to be selected by a team in the draft as the sixth overall pick of the Oklahoma City Thunder.

He joined a record 125 international players from across 40 countries on opening night in 2023. Inevitably, many came from Canada, but there were representatives from Europe – a traditional NBA hunting ground – in the form of French, German, Serbian and Turkish players. Players from foreign climes aren't just benchwarmers either. In recent years, the NBA has been privileged to host MVPs Giannis Antetokounmpo (Greece) and Nikola Jokic (Serbia), All-Stars Domantas Sabonis (Lithuania) and Luka Doncic (Slovenia), and rising star Victor Wembanyama (France).

55

THE GOLDEN BOY

Few players revolutionised the NBA in the way that **Stephen Curry** did. He was drafted in the first round by the Golden State Warriors in 2009, and his new team hoped they'd get a face of the franchise. They got that and more. Curry redefined the point guard role. As well as bringing he ball up and distributing it to teammates to score, Curry was just as happy to shoot from distance – and boy, was he good at it. His field goal percentage never sank below .400 during the first 14 years of his career, and even breached .504 in 2015-16. That same year, Curry also had a league-leading 30.1 points per game and 5.1 three-pointers per game.

He earned his second consecutive MVP award for those phenomenal stats and has led the Warriors to four NBA titles. Curry's better-than .900 free-throw percentage is an all-time NBA record, and in November 2023, he reached a new milestone of hitting a three-pointer in 250 consecutive games – that's every game three seasons on the trot. Simply the greatest long-distance shooter the league has ever seen, Curry can even hit baskets from the centre circle.

56

ROCK THE BABY

Julius Erving was one of the NBA's first great entertainers, and his most memorable move was a slam dunk against the Los Angeles Lakers in 1983. Irving ran for the basket with only Michael Cooper to beat on defence and went for a spectacular score. He jumped right after the foul line, and as he sailed to the basket, rocked the ball in his giant hand as though rocking the cradle before slamming it into the basket. Cooper could do little else but duck out of the way and admit that he'd just been beaten by the greatest dunk of all time.

MLK DAY

★★★★★★★★★★★★

As a league with a high proportion of Black players, it's fitting that the NBA schedules a top-quality schedule on the third Monday of January, better known as **Martin Luther King Jr Day**. Usually, the matchups feature a playoff rematch, and where possible, King's hometown Atlanta Hawks are a home team. After the Vancouver Grizzlies relocated in 2001 to Memphis, the scene of King's assassination, they also began hosting games. The Hawks seem to be particularly inspired by King's memory and have one of the best win percentages in MLK Day games since the public holiday was introduced in 1986.

57

58

THE SHOT CLOCK

George Mikan and his Minneapolis Lakers were so dominant in the early days of the NBA that opposing teams could only find one way to stop them: kill the game. They kept the score as low as possible and hoped to nick points on counterattacks, a strategy that reached an extreme on 22 November 1950 when the Fort Wayne Pistons beat the Lakers 19-18. The Pistons passed the ball between themselves for minutes at a time and attempted only 13 shots all game. A few weeks later, the Rochester Royals and Indianapolis Olympians played a six-overtime game during which both teams attempted the same tactic: hold the ball for the whole of overtime and attempt a shot in the dying seconds.

To prevent such suffocating tactics turning away fans, the NBA came up with the **shot clock** in 1954. Under the new rules, teams had only 24 seconds to take a shot, otherwise they lost possession. The effect was almost instantaneous. The average points per game went from 79 in 1953-54 to 93 in 1954-55 and 107 by 1957-58. Thanks to the shot clock, the modern NBA is far removed from the stifling game-killing tactics of the early years.

59

THE DREAM TEAM

★★★★★★★★★★★★★★★★★★★★★★★★★

The USA unsurprisingly dominated basketball at the Olympic Games after it was introduced in 1936, winning ten of the first 13 gold medals – but since pro players were not allowed to compete, Team USA tended to be represented by college athletes. That changed at the Barcelona Games in 1992, after the International Basketball Federation changed the rules to allow NBA players to compete. USA Basketball immediately picked a team of superstars that has gone down in history as the **Dream Team**.

It included not only a host of future Hall of Famers, but many of the greatest players to ever grace the court: Michael Jordan, Larry Bird, Scottie Pippen and Charles Barkley. Even Magic Johnson came out of retirement for one last whirl. Given the star-studded nature of the team, the 1992 basketball gold medal was perhaps the easiest prediction in Olympic history. The Dream Team began with a 116-48 demolition of Angola before seeing off six other teams en-route to the gold medal game. That one was no closer when USA gave a 117-85 beatdown to Croatia. Team USA had an average plus-44 points differential and the entire team was inducted into the Hall of Fame.

60

THE GODFATHER

★★★★★★★★★★★★★★★★★★★★

Although he's known as the Godfather for his sharp suits and slicked-back hair, **Pat Riley** ruled the franchises he coached like a gang boss too – and his approach brought results. He won four titles with the Showtime-era Los Angeles Lakers between 1982 and 1988 before moving on to the New York Knicks and Miami Heat. Riley's perseverance in Florida was rewarded with a fifth championship in 2006, and he won the Coach of the Year awards at all three coaching stops. He remained in Miami as president of the Heat and has built two-more championship-winning teams from the front office.

IN-SEASON TOURNAMENT

To give the long slog of regular season games more immediate impact, the NBA introduced a new feature for the 2023-24 season – an **In-Season Tournament** that ran alongside the regular season schedule in November and December. Each team was put into a five-team group. One regular season game against each opponent doubled up as a tournament game, and the best teams progressed to the knockout stages. By the time the first NBA Cup was awarded to the Los Angeles Lakers, it wasn't just LeBron and his teammates celebrating – NBA bosses were also ecstatic. Stadium attendance and television viewing figures were up, as was media interest.

61

62

SCORING SHOOTING GUARDS

★★★★★★★★★★★★★★★★★★★★

Points, points, points: a shooting guard's main priority is to keep the scoreboard ticking over with regular baskets. Some choose to hang back and shoot from distance, and a decent NBA shooting guard will hit the basket more than a third of the time from beyond the three-point line. Others like to drive at the basket and put defenders on the back foot, leaping for lay-ups and impressive slam dunks. Opponents may try to negate the effect of the shooting guard by double-teaming them, but this can backfire if the guard is a good ball-handler who can distribute it for assists.

Instead, most teams use their shooting guard to mark the other team's shooting guard, and these one-on-one matchups often decide the result of a game. Combo guards add an extra element to the mix by rotating with the point guard to bring the ball up the court. When a game goes down to the wire and a team needs a score with seconds on the clock, they'll usually run a play that gets the shooting guard in position to take a clutch jump shot – a tactic that's led to iconic moments for players like Michael Jordan and **Kobe Bryant** sealing the win.

63

THE DECISION

LeBron James is rightly acclaimed as one of the greatest NBA players of all time, but not everything in his career went to plan. His first departure from the team that drafted him could certainly have been handled better. As his contract ran out and James hit free agency, there was no shortage of suitors. He decided to announce the next stop in his basketball journey in a live television special broadcast on ESPN. *The Decision*, as the show was titled, was little more than a vanity project.

Special guests were invited to gush over James's unnatural talent, and after teasing his audience for over an hour, he finally revealed that he'd accepted an offer from the Miami Heat – but the Cleveland Cavaliers were only informed just before the programme aired. 'This is a business and I had seven great years in Cleveland,' James declared. 'I hope the fans understand; maybe they won't.' They didn't. Cavs fans vowed never to forgive him for his public snub, though most did when James returned after four seasons and led the Cavs to an NBA title. Neutral fans were underwhelmed by the spectacle, and sportswriters competed to condemn James for acting as though he was bigger than the sport.

THE DREAM

Hakeem 'The Dream' Olajuwon was the first pick of the 1984 NBA Draft, a selection that put him ahead of Michael Jordan. Although the Houston Rockets may have regretted missing out on Jordan, they couldn't complain too much since they did get a tremendous centre. Olajuwon redefined the centre role, playing in a much more offensive manner compared to his predecessors. After Jordan retired for the first time in 1993, Olajuwon finally moved out from under his shadow. He was named NBA MVP in 1994 and led the Rockets to successive NBA titles in 1994 and 1995.

STEALS

★★★★★★★★★★

Stealing the ball requires good anticipation and razor-sharp reflexes. A great stealer pounces to nick the ball when an opponent is mid-dribble and, even if an attempt doesn't pay off, it often forces an attacker to pause and mis-time a play. Stealing is usually the speciality of small, quick guards, but not always, and seven-foot centre Hakeem Olajuwon ranks in the list of all-time top ten stealers. Utah Jazz point guard **John Stockton** was better than anybody. He dispossessed his opponents 3,265 times during his career, more than 500 times more than the next-best stealer.

65

66

ALL-STAR BREAK

★★★★★★★★★★★★★★★★★★★

In the middle of the regular season, when bodies are tired and muscles are aching, most NBA players benefit from a few days' rest – but not if you're judged to be one of the best. The league's top players are selected for the **All-Star Game**, an exhibition that features the 24 top performers, usually in the form of Eastern Conference v Western Conference. Starting line-ups are chosen through a combination of fan, player and media voting, while the benches are chosen by head coaches. The All-Star Game is much less competitive than a regular encounter.

Players compete to score the most spectacular baskets as much as they do to win the game, and an extended half-time allows for a mini-concert by popular artists. Aside from the main event, the All-Star break also features the Slam Dunk Contest, Three-Point Contest, Skills Challenge and a Rising Stars Challenge for first- and second-year players. It also has the celebrity game, in which some competitors reveal a surprising talent for the game, like Secretary of Education Arne Duncan and five-feet four-inch comedian Kevin Hart. When the festivities are over and the All-Star break ends, it's back to the regular season and the playoff chase really begins.

67

LARRY LEGEND

Larry Bird made an immediate impact on the NBA after he was drafted by the Boston Celtics in 1978. He refused to sign a sub-par contract and played hardball, only committing to the team when they made him the highest-paid rookie in sports history. The tough negotiating style signalled what the Celtics were about to get: a phenomenally determined man who had an unrivalled will to win. Bird benefited from the introduction of the three-point line in 1979 and soon proved to be a fantastic shooter.

In 1986-87 he entered the select 50-40-90 club when he shot .525 from the field, .400 from three-point range and .910 on free throws. After that, back injuries began to take their toll, and Bird eventually retired early after the 1992 season. The Celtics would miss their talisman. During his final two seasons, they were 71-28 when he played and 30-29 when he did not. Bird's 13-year career saw him win three NBA rings and three MVP awards, and he's the only person in league history to be named Rookie of the Year, NBA MVP, Finals MVP, All-Star MVP, Coach of the Year and Executive of the Year.

68

LINSANITY

★★★★★★★★★★★★★★

For a couple of weeks in February 2012, **Jeremy Lin's** remarkable rise was the talk of the NBA. The undrafted player struggled to get a secure spot on an NBA roster, but the New York Knicks claimed him off waivers as injury cover in late 2011. They found a diamond in the rough. Lin scored, assisted and rebounded like an All-Star, spurring the Knicks into a seven-game win streak. Sadly, despite a big-money contract from the Houston Rockets during the offseason, Lin never reached the same heights again and he returned to being a benchwarmer until he left the NBA in 2019.

SLEEP SCIENCE

In the search for marginal gains that might make the difference between a one-point win and a one-point loss, NBA teams are prepared to leave no stone unturned. One recent area of interest is what players get up to in bed. Since players spend a lot of time on the road, they lay their heads in many different hotels. Now, teams employ **sleep** specialists who analyse the quality of players' rest through wearable devices and plan travel itineraries to avoid night-time journeys. Thanks to this research, the NBA has proven that the old adage is wrong – if you snooze, you *don't* lose.

70

RIVALRIES

Some teams face each other so often in crunch matchups that they become fed up with each other. That happened to the New York Knicks and Miami Heat in the late 1990s, when they met in the playoffs for four straight years. Every game was full of niggles and aggressive defence, and there was no love lost between Knicks lynchpin Patrick Ewing and Heat legend Alonzo Mourning. Knicks coach Pat Riley didn't mind the Heat, however. He left New York to coach in Miami in 1995, and his resignation letter was sent by fax.

The Chicago Bulls and Detroit Pistons also regularly clashed in the 1990s, as did the Cleveland Cavaliers and Golden State Warriors in the 2010s, but no teams did rivalry better than the **Los Angeles Lakers** and **Boston Celtics** in the 1980s. Boston was an East Coast, predominantly white city with Larry Bird as its talisman. West Coast LA was more racially diverse and featured Magic Johnson as its star. Today, the NBA takes advantage of its historic rivalries by having its schedule organisers designate a spot in the calendar for Rivals Week, when many of the most notorious matchups take place.

71

MAGIC

One of the few sports stars who became so famous that he's known by his nickname rather than his given name, **Earvin 'Magic' Johnson** joined luminaries like Tiger Woods and Babe Ruth thanks to a celebrated career with the Los Angeles Lakers that saw him gain five NBA titles and three MVP awards. Six-feet nine-inch Johnson was incredibly tall for a point guard, and his height gave him great court vision. Thanks to his superb playmaking, Johnson still holds the all-time NBA record for assists per game in the regular season and postseason. Johnson's years in the NBA coincided with Larry Bird.

The two Hall of Famers were both drafted in 1979, and they played out one of the NBA's best-known rivalries, but away from the court, they were friends. Just like Bird, Johnson was forced into early retirement, although Johnson's announcement was prompted by a diagnosis of HIV resulting from unprotected sex. Johnson had two short returns to the NBA and formed a touring exhibition team. He also dedicated much of his time to helping fundraise to find a cure, and is credited with raising awareness of how HIV isn't just a disease that strikes gay men and drug-users.

72

THE HALF-COURT SHOT

★★★★★★★★

The likelihood of a long-distance shot succeeding in the NBA is so low that only a few hundred are attempted every year. Sometimes, there's no choice. **Jerry West** found himself in that situation in Game 3 of the 1970 NBA Finals. His Los Angeles Lakers were two points down with time almost gone, so West launched a shot from 60 feet – and it went in. Since there were no three-pointers, the game went to overtime, and the fairy-tale ending never happened – the Lakers failed to capitalise on West's half-court shot and lost the game.

PLAY-IN TOURNAMENT

The NBA playoffs begin with a bang: a pre-playoff featuring the franchises that finish from seventh to tenth in each conference at the end of the regular season standings. These four teams are pitched against each other to decide the final two seedings for each conference, and the win-or-go-home elimination format makes for some spectacular games like the Los Angeles Lakers' overtime win against the Minnesota Timberwolves in 2023. The **Play-In Tournament** arose from necessity during the Covid-19 pandemic, but proved so effective at keeping the last few regular season games as meaningful encounters that it was retained when the world returned to normal.

74

UNIFORMS

The original NBA uniforms were plain: a simple **vest** featuring the team's name and player's number. Durability was the name of the game, with thick polyester vests and belted shorts. Colours became much more vibrant in the 1960s and 1970s. Uniforms began to feature bold stripes, socks became longer and headbands held back long hair. The 1980s was the era of experimentation. Michael Jordan asked his kit manufacturer to make his shorts longer in 1987 and some teams tried out V-shaped necks. One part of the kit that didn't change was footwear.

When Jordan entered the league, sneakers had to be more than half white or half black with just a simple colour accent – a rule that he fell foul of when his signature red-and-black Air Jordans were launched in 1984, but which Nike took full advantage of when it came to creating publicity. Only in 2018 were players allowed to wear sneakers of any colour in any game. Now, players wear breathable, lightweight, high-tech fabrics designed in consultation with the players' association. The Golden State Warriors became the first team to try out sleeved jerseys in 2013, but to the relief of basketball fans everywhere, they didn't catch on.

75

THE BLOCK

Probably the greatest defensive clutch play in NBA history occurred when the 2016 NBA Finals went down to the wire. In the closing minutes of the deciding Game 7, with the Cleveland Cavaliers seeking their first title and tied with the Golden State Warriors at 89 apiece, Cavs guard Kyrie Irving tried to float the ball into the basket. He missed. Warriors forward Andre Iguodala snaffled the ball and went for a fast break with only one defender between him and the Cavaliers basket. Iguodala exchanged passes with Stephen Curry to wrong-foot the defender and went for a simple lay-up to put the Warriors ahead, but the ball was blocked by **LeBron James**, who appeared out of nowhere to jam the ball against the backboard.

Analysts later concluded that James reached 20 miles per hour in his chase-down, and the ball fell back into Cavalier hands with the scores still tied. With less than two minutes to go, the wind seemed to go out of the Warriors' sails. Irving hit a three-pointer to put the Cavaliers ahead, and it was fitting that James scored the final point of the game from the free-throw line after his remarkable game-changing block.

76

THE ROUND MOUND OF REBOUND

Though six-foot six-inch **Charles Barkley** was shorter than a typical power forward, he was a brilliant rebounder. He used his strength and determination to snaffle balls that really shouldn't have been his, and that same strength and determination often got him into confrontations with opponents, officials, and occasionally fans. An All-Star every year between 1987 and 1997, he was named MVP in 1993 while playing with the Phoenix Suns. Though a regular in the playoffs, Barkley never won a championship ring. The closest he came was his MVP season, when the Suns lost to the Chicago Bulls in six games.

NUMBER ONE DRAFT BUSTS

★★★★★★★★★★★★★★★★★

Getting the first pick in the draft isn't a guarantee of success. **Greg Oden** was supposed to become the face of the Portland Trail Blazers when he was drafted first overall in 2007 (ahead of future Hall of Famer Kevin Durant) but knee injuries meant that Oden played just 105 games over six seasons. At least Oden lasted six years. Anthony Bennett was selected number one by the Cleveland Cavaliers in 2013 but was traded after just one season and was out of the NBA by the age of 23. Not top picks are busts, though. LeBron James, Magic Johnson and Shaquille O'Neal worked out after they were chosen first in their respective drafts.

78
SLAM DUNKS
SPALDING

No move is more of a crowd-pleaser than the slam dunk – where a player jumps to the basket and shoves the ball through the rim with one or two hands. It's a high-percentage shot that almost guarantees two points – so much so that the phrase has entered general usage as a sure thing – although defences will try to prevent dunk attempts by physically guarding the basket and laying their bodies on the line to block a run. The term arose in pre-NBA days, when a journalist described the shot as like 'a cafeteria customer dunking a roll in coffee'.

Early NBA stars knew there was a chance of retribution if they embarrassed their opponent with too many dunks, but dunks became increasingly common thanks to tall centres like Bill Russell and Wilt Chamberlain making it part of their arsenal. The NBA cottoned on to its popularity with a Slam Dunk Contest during the All-Star break in 1984 (though the ABA had an earlier Slam Dunk Contest during half-time of its 1976 All-Star Game). Journeyman point guard **Nate Robinson** has won the most Slam Dunk Contests with three, while Shaquille O'Neal, Vince Carter and LeBron James earned reputations as some of the best game-time dunkers.

79

THE FLU GAME

Michael Jordan spent the day leading up to Game 5 of the 1997 NBA Finals locked in his hotel room, and it wasn't a pretty sight. He lay curled up in the foetal position in between trips to the toilet to vomit or have diarrhoea. Jordan was likely suffering the after effects of a dodgy pizza he ate the night before, and medics told him to stay in his room and get ready for Game 6 instead. But Jordan wasn't having any of that. He dragged himself out of bed at 5.50 p.m. ahead of the 7 o'clock tip off at the Utah Jazz's Delta Centre.

He missed warming up – an absence explained to the media as due to flu-like symptoms – and was sluggish when the game began, but Jordan slowly got into his groove in a close game. In the fourth quarter, he was back to his normal self. He tied the game with a free throw and made a three-pointer to put the Bulls in the lead with 25 seconds remaining. When the game finally ended, Jordan collapsed into **Scottie Pippen's** arms, an iconic image that summed up what became known as the Flu Game, though it'd be more accurate to call it the Food Poisoning Game.

80

ICEMAN

Steve Kerr already had a full hand of NBA rings when he retired as a player – three with the Chicago Bulls and two with the San Antonio Spurs – but he added to his haul with another four gained as head coach of the Golden State Warriors. As a coach, Kerr combined the triangle offense of Phil Jackson's Bulls and the speed employed of Gregg Popovich's Spurs into his own style of play. In recent years, Kerr has encouraged Stephen Curry to play as a points-scoring point guard to make his team near-undefendable.

PUNISHING POWER FORWARDS

Something of a mini-centre, the power forward must help secure the ball by grabbing rebounds and defending the basket. Some are dismissed as 'tweeners' – wannabe centres who don't have the height – but a specialist power forward gives their team extra options on both offense and defence, and great power forwards like Tim Duncan or **Dennis Rodman** are willing to put their body on the line, diving for loose balls and fighting for rebounds. Although a power forward rarely gains the headlines, they're the workhorses whose selfless work carries a team to victory.

82

PLAYOFFS

The business end to the season begins when the playoffs roll around. Only the 16 best teams progress from the regular season and play-in tournament. They're matched up based on regular season performance into best-of-seven series: the number one seed in each conference plays number eight from the same conference, seed two plays seed seven, seed three plays seed six, and seeds four and five face off. From there, the brackets are set. The winner of 1v8 plays the winner of 4v5, and the winner of 2v7 plays the winner of 3v6. It all progresses to two teams competing in the Conference Finals, and the two conference champions meeting in the NBA Finals.

Only six eighth-seeded teams have ever beaten the number-one seed, and none have ever won the overall title. Nor has a seventh seed – the 1995 sixth-seed Houston Rockets are the lowest-ranked team to go all the way through the playoffs. No team has ever gone undefeated, but the **Golden State Warriors** have the best record since the current system was put in place. They won the 2017 title by winning 16 postseason contests and losing only one – the penultimate game of the Finals.

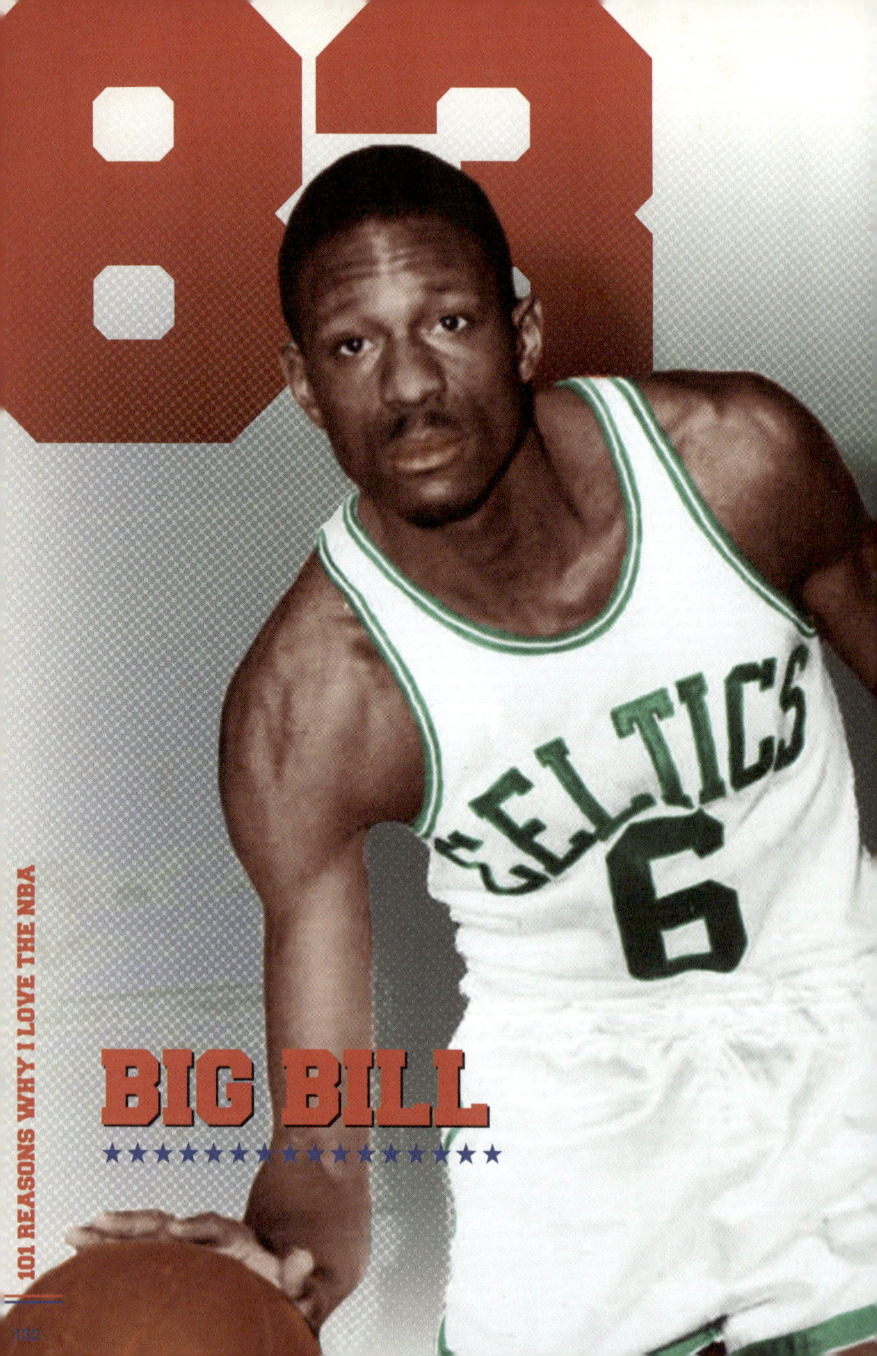

83

BIG BILL

The St Louis Hawks made a legendary mistake after the 1956 draft. They selected a young centre named **Bill Russell**, but had their sights set on Boston Celtics' six-time All-Star centre Ed Macauley. They offered the Celtics a trade – the young prospect for the established star – and the Celtics said yes. Macauley was no slouch, but Russell soon proved to be a far superior player. Though he never set the world alight on offense, he was probably the NBA's greatest-ever defender, and as the old adage goes, defence wins championships.

It certainly did in Russell's case. In his 13-year NBA career, the Celtics won the NBA title on an outrageous 11 occasions – and the two times they didn't, they were the losing Finalists. Russell led the league in rebounding four times and picked up five MVP awards. He was a pioneer of race relations in the NBA too. He was the sport's first Black superstar, the first Black head coach (in a city that wasn't renowned for embracing Black sports stars), and his number-six vest has been retired across the league. He also sported one of the greatest laughs of all time – the kind of chuckle that is contagious to anybody who hears it.

84

THE FIRST GAME

When **Ossie Schectman** took a pass to score a basket for the New York Knickerbockers against the Toronto Huskies on 1 November 1946, it was more than just the game's first basket. It was the first ever score in a new league, the Basketball Association of America. Set up by the entrepreneurial owners of ice hockey arenas in the Northeast and Midwest, who wanted an extra income stream from their property, the new league proved super popular. In 1949, after merging with the failing National Basketball League, the BAA was renamed to the more familiar NBA.

ANNIVERSARY TEAMS

The NBA has named four teams to mark significant milestones: 25, 35, 50 and 75 years since its inception. The idea began with as an All-NBA team of players who'd retired by the 1971 season: four guards, four forwards and two centres. The teams that came after didn't stick to the same criteria. In the 35th-year team, an eleventh player was added and two active players made the cut. By the 50th anniversary, the roster had ballooned to 50 players. By the **75th anniversary**, thanks to a tie in the voting for the last place, it was 76.

86

TEAM NAMES

From the Chicago Bulls to the Golden State Warriors, the NBA is stuffed with iconic nicknames. Most derive from the early days of the team. The Boston Celtics are named for their city's Irish ancestry, but they were nearly the Olympians, Whirlwinds or Unicorns. The Milwaukee Bucks were almost the Robins, but the team's owner overruled the public's choice. At least they didn't go with the next-best option, the Skunks. The most recent NBA franchise was going to be the Charlotte Spirit, but fans hated the name.

A poll decided on Hornets over the other four options: Cougars, Crowns, Knights and Stars. Not all nicknames make sense at first glance. Los Angeles isn't known for its lakes – but the Lakers name derives from the team's original home, Minneapolis, the City of Lakes. Memphis doesn't have any grizzlies, but the team was first established in Vancouver. Not every team has retained its original moniker. The **Denver Nuggets** were originally the Rockets but had to change since that name was already taken by Houston when the ABA and NBA merged. The Buffalo Braves changed to the San Diego Clippers when they relocated in 1978, but they kept the nickname when they shifted again to Los Angeles in 1984.

87
BLACK MAMBA
LAKERS
24
SPALDING

Kobe Bryant rose to international fame posthumously, when he was killed in a helicopter crash with his daughter Gianna in 2020. By that time, Bryant had been retired from the NBA for four years, but basketball fans still missed his signature moves. A shooting guard who mimicked Michael Jordan in playing style, Bryant favoured a fade-away jump shot (a shot taken while jumping backwards to create space) and was renowned for his ability to win games in the dying seconds, even if he was double-or triple-teamed by opponents who knew his ability in clutch situations.

Lakers fans loved him, and he repaid them by spending his entire career in Los Angeles. Other teams' fans loved to boo him, although Bryant often revelled in playing the villain and silencing hostile crowds with his play – like his 81-point game against the Toronto Raptors in 2006. Though an 18-time All-Star and five-time NBA champion, Bryant was surprisingly only voted MVP once, in 2008. He formed a formidable duo with Shaquille O'Neal and helped the Lakers to a three-peat between 2000 and 2002, even though the two didn't really get along, and followed up with an almost-as-good partnership with Spanish power forward Pau Gasol.

88

THE RIVALS

The high point of the NBA's greatest rivalry came in the 1984 Finals, when **Larry Bird's** Boston Celtics went toe-to-toe with **Magic Johnson's** Los Angeles Lakers. The 'Showtime' Lakers were 2-1 up after three games and took a ten-point lead into half-time in Game 4, but the hard-nosed, physical Celtics didn't give in and ground down their opponents. The Celtics came from behind to win in overtime, and the momentum swung to the Bostonians as they went on to win the championship. Bird's monster Game 4 of 29 points and 21 rebounds solidified his reputation as the most ruthlessly competitive player in NBA history.

Most fans agree that Michael Jordan is the best player in NBA history, so it's fitting that the player chosen as the season's Most Valuable Player is awarded the Michael Jordan Trophy. Jordan was named MVP on five occasions, although Kareem Abdul-Jabbar got one more with six. Jabbar's awards all came during the era when players voted for the MVP, but since 1980, a panel of writers and broadcasters chooses the winner. Stephen Curry is the only person to have been a unanimous choice, while Wilt Chamberlain and **Wes Unseld** are the only rookie winners.

89

THE LOGO

In 1969, the NBA commissioner decided he wanted a new logo fashioned on Major League Baseball's white silhouette on a red and blue background. Designer Alan Siegel looked through countless images of basketball players and settled on one of a player dribbling past an opponent. Siegel knocked up a rough example, showed it to the commissioner, and the job was done. It took about 30 minutes. Since then, the NBA logo has become one of sport's most globally recognised emblems. It's dynamic, instantly recognisable, and gives the impression of a fast-moving sport.

Only later did Siegel reveal that Los Angeles Lakers guard **Jerry West** was the basis of his design. During his 14-year career with the Lakers, West aka 'The Logo' scored over 25,000 points and led the Lakers in scoring in seven different seasons. He won one NBA title in 1972, but it could have been a lot more. Thanks to the dominance of Bill Russell and Wilt Chamberlain, West's Lakers were on the losing side in seven different Finals. Although he isn't as famous as other legends of the sport, thanks to the NBA logo, everyone instantly recognises West's silhouette – even if they don't know who he is.

91

BREAKING THE COLOUR BARRIER

When the NBA was first formed as the Basketball Association of America in 1946, it was – like all pro sports in the United States during this era – a white man's sport. Many sports fans know that Jackie Robinson broke baseball's colour line in 1947, but later that year, Japanese American **Wataru Misaka** broke basketball's colour barrier when he played for the New York Knicks. Misaka couldn't hold down a permanent place and was cut after three games, and he remained the only non-white player in the league until the Washington Capitols signed Harold Hunter, a Black American, in 1950.

Though Hunter was cut before the season began, several other teams followed the Capitols' example and signed Black players. Chuck Cooper made his debut for the Boston Celtics on 1 November 1950, Nathaniel 'Sweetwater' Clifton turned out for the New York Knicks three days later, but the Capitols signed a Black player who beat them both to it: future Hall of Famer Earl Lloyd debuted on 31 October. Now, thanks to these trailblazing pioneers, three-quarters of NBA players are Black and the NBA is the most diverse North American pro sports league.

92

THE JOKER

★★★★★★★★★★★★★★

Six-foot eleven-inch **Nikola Jokic** was always going to stand head and shoulders above his peers – and that's even the case in the NBA, where the Serbian centre won the MVP award in 2021, 2022 and 2024. Even though he didn't pick up the best player going into 2023, he did lead the Denver Nuggets into their first NBA championship. Not everybody expected Jokic to be such a stud. He was drafted by the Nuggets in 2014 in the second round on the 41st pick, meaning that every franchise initially passed on the chance to have him, and Jokic is the lowest-drafted player to win the MVP award.

THE LARRY O'BRIEN TROPHY

The first 37 winners of the NBA Finals were awarded the Walter A. Brown Trophy, named after the founder of the Boston Celtics. In 1984, the championship trophy was renamed in honour of **Larry O'Brien**, who retired earlier that year as NBA Commissioner, having seen the sport through a decade of growth. Tiffany's manufactures a new trophy for each year's NBA championship-winning team, and winning franchises proudly display their two-feet tall mementoes of their success – and at the time of writing, nobody has more on display than the Boston Celtics, who have won the title 18 times.

94

CHASE-DOWNS

Basketball statisticians have always recorded who scores the most baskets, but defensively minded players had to wait until 1973 for the NBA to begin recording who blocked the most shots. This vital part of the game is an art form itself. The blocker – typically a tall centre or power forward – must try to deflect a shot as it makes it to the basket, but without touching the shooter's hand or touching the ball after it reaches the top of its arc and begins to drop.

The most stunning blocks of all are chase-downs, when a defender races after an opponent who's gotten away on a fast break. If the breaker attempts a lay-up, the blocker must try to divert the ball against the backboard. When it works, it looks spectacular. **Tayshaun Prince** saved the Detroit Pistons in the last moments of Game 2 of the Eastern Conference Finals with an epic chase-down of Indiana Pacers' **Reggie Miller**. Prince blocked Miller's lay-up and his momentum carried him into the third row of spectators. LeBron James's effort against Andre Iguodala in the deciding game of the 2016 NBA Finals has gone down in basketball lore as 'The Block'.

THE MAGIC TOUCH

The 1980 NBA Finals featuring the Los Angeles Lakers and Philadelphia 76ers was a delicately balanced affair. No team won by more than ten points during the first five games. The Lakers went into Game 6 with a 3-2 lead but a black cloud hanging over them. MVP Kareem Abdul-Jabbar had sprained his ankle in Game 5 and was quickly ruled out by the team doctor. Jabbar was averaging 33.4 points in the series, and few gave the Lakers a chance without him, but rather than swap out their talisman for a reserve centre, head coach Paul Westhead tried something nobody was expecting. He asked six-foot nine-inch point guard **Magic Johnson** to step into Jabbar's shoes.

Lakers fans groaned as Johnson lost the opening tip, but he soon recovered and put in the performance of his career. The 20-year-old rookie showed no sign of nerves as he racked up 42 points, 15 rebounds, seven assists, three steals and a block in one of the most dominant displays in Finals history. The Lakers won 123-107 and won the championship title without Jabbar, and Johnson even nicked the Finals MVP away from his injured centre thanks to one extraordinary game.

96

ROBIN

Scottie Pippen only ever led the league in one stat category (steals in 1994-95), but he ended his career with six NBA rings because he was the perfect support act to Michael Jordan at the Chicago Bulls. As Robin to Jordan's Batman, Pippen was an elite perimeter defender who prevented opponents from scoring and put the ball in Jordan's hands to let him do his thing. Pippen topped 20 points per game four times between 1991 and 1997, averaged five-plus rebounds and five-plus assists every year from 1989 to 2000, and was selected to the All-Star roster on seven different occasions.

MADISON SQUARE GARDEN

★★★★★★★★★★★★★★★★★★★★★

One of the most famous sports venues in the world, the current **Madison Square Gardens** in New York is the fourth iteration. Built over the top of Penn Station, the latest Garden was designed as the home venue of the New York Knicks and NHL franchise the New York Rangers. Aside from hosting the championship-winning Knicks sides of 1970 and 1973, Madison Square Gardens was the location of Stephen Curry's record-breaking 2,977th three-pointer, saw Muhammad Ali fight Joe Frazier in 'the Fight of the Century', and is the second-highest-grossing music venue in terms of ticket sales.

98

THE FINALS

There can be only one champion at the end of the season, and the best team rises to the top at the end of each spring in the NBA Finals, the showpiece best-of-seven series between the Eastern Conference champion and Western Conference champion. Since there's likely to be cross-country travel involved, the Finals follows a 2-3-2 format in which the team with the best regular season record has the first and last games. The **Lakers** dominate the list of most Finals appearances. Whether based in Minneapolis or Los Angeles, they've reached the Finals 32 times as of 2024, more than nine appearances ahead of their nearest rivals, the Boston Celtics – but the **Celtics** have a far superior win percentage.

Several teams are in the unfortunate position of never winning the Finals despite making the big game, including the Chicago Stags and Washington Capitols. Neither will ever get the chance to make up for their Finals loss, since both franchises have subsequently folded. The Utah Jazz have never won a championship title either, though they did feature in the most-viewed NBA Finals of all time: the 1987 series between the Chicago Bulls and Utah Jazz was watched by an average 29 million viewers on US television.

99

COACH POP

Gregg Popovich must be overflowing with self-confidence. Popovich was a former college coach and NBA assistant before he was appointed general manager of the San Antonio Spurs in 1994, and two years later, the Spurs found themselves needing a new head coach. Despite never playing in the NBA nor being a head coach in the big league, Popovich appointed himself to the job. The bold move paid off quickly. From sixth in the Midwest Division in his first season, the Spurs climbed to second in his second campaign and were NBA champions at the end of his third.

The Spurs got another three titles in a five-year stretch from 2003 to 2007, and another in 2014. Popovich adapted his strategy and gameplan to the players available to him rather than sticking to one style, and it served him well for an extended period. His first 22 seasons were winning seasons (an NBA record), with 21 consecutive playoff appearances (another NBA record) and a career total of more than 1,375 games won (yes, an NBA record). Although the Spurs fell off dramatically after they missed out on the playoffs in 2020, Coach Pop's place in the Hall of Fame was already secure.

100

THE LAST DANCE

★★★★★★★★★★★★★★★★★★★★★

In the spring of 2020, as country after country went into lockdown to stop the spread of Covid-19, the world's population found themselves stuck at home with nothing to do. Though the pandemic was an international tragedy, it was perfect timing for the launch of a documentary series on Netflix. ***The Last Dance*** focused on Michael Jordan's final year with the Chicago Bulls, but its attention roved over his whole career and featured interviews with many teammates and NBA personalities. The program attracted many new fans, many of whom would never previously have considered basketball as a sport of interest.

SUMMER LEAGUE

After the season comes to an end, starving NBA fans don't have to wait long until their next fix. Less than a month later, the **Summer League** begins in Las Vegas, with other affiliated summer leagues in Salt Lake City and California. Teams use the summer league to try out different rosters. Superstars tend to be rested, but the Summer League is a great chance to blood new talent from the draft, promote G League players, or give veterans an opportunity to rehabilitate after injury. And after the Summer League finishes, it's only three months until the NBA season begins once again.

About the Author

Scott Reeves is an award-winning sportswriter who has authored seven books and contributed to several guides to the NBA, NFL and college football.

He lives in Shropshire and is an avid follower of the Boston Celtics and NewEngland Patriots.

Photography courtesy of

Getty images, Alamy and Wiki Commons